The Shakespe

THE SHAKESPEARE HANDBOOKS

Series Editor: John Russell Brown

PUBLISHED

John Russell Brown	*Macbeth*
Paul Edmondson	*Twelfth Night*
Christopher McCullough	*The Merchant of Venice*
Lesley Wade Soule	*As You Like It*

FORTHCOMING

Roger Apfelbaum	*Much Ado About Nothing*
John Russell Brown	*Hamlet*
David Carnegie	*Julius Caesar*
Bridget Escolme	*Antony and Cleopatra*
Kevin Ewert	*Henry V*
Trevor Griffiths	*The Tempest*
Stuart Hampton-Reeves	*Measure for Measure*
Margaret Jane Kidnie	*The Taming of the Shrew*
Paul Prescott	*Richard III*
Edward L. Rocklin	*Romeo and Juliet*
Martin White	*A Midsummer Night's Dream*

The Shakespeare Handbooks

As You Like It

Lesley Wade Soule

First published 2005 by
PALGRAVE MACMILLAN
Houndmills, Basingstoke, Hampshire RG21 6XS and
175 Fifth Avenue, New York, N.Y. 10010
Companies and representatives throughout the world

PALGRAVE MACMILLAN is the global academic imprint of the Palgrave Macmillan division of St. Martin's Press, LLC and of Palgrave Macmillan Ltd. Macmillan® is a registered trademark in the United States, United Kingdom and other countries. Palgrave is a registered trademark in the European Union and other countries.

ISBN-13: 978–1–4039–3630–1 hardback
ISBN 10: 1–4039–3630–7   hardback
ISBN-13: 978–1–4039–3629–5 paperback
ISBN 10: 1–4039–3629–3   paperback

This book is printed on paper suitable for recycling and made from fully managed and sustained forest sources.

A catalogue record for this book is available from the British Library.

A catalog record for this book is available from the Library Congress.

10	9	8	7	6	5	4	3	2	1
14	13	12	11	10	09	08	07	06	05

Printed and bound in China

Contents

General Editor's Preface

The Shakespeare Handbooks provide an innovative way of studying the theatrical life of the plays. The commentaries, which are their core feature, enable a reader to envisage the words of a text unfurling in performance, involving actions and meanings not readily perceived except in rehearsal or performance. The aim is to present the plays in the environment for which they were written and to offer an experience as close as possible to an audience's progressive experience of a production.

While each book has the same range of contents, their authors have been encouraged to shape them according to their own critical and scholarly understanding and their first-hand experience of theatre practice. The various chapters are designed to complement the commentaries: the cultural context of each play is presented together with quotations from original sources; the authority of its text or texts is considered with what is known of the earliest performances; key performances and productions of its subsequent stage history are both described and compared. The aim in all this has been to help readers to develop their own informed and imaginative view of a play in ways that supplement the provision of standard editions and are more user-friendly than detailed stage histories or collections of criticism from diverse sources.

Further volumes are in preparation so that, within a few years, the Shakespeare Handbooks will be available for all the plays that are frequently studied and performed.

John Russell Brown
January 2005

Preface

A useful image for approaching *As You Like It* as a theatrical experience is the space created by the great German director Peter Stein for his production of the play. For the Forest of Arden, he and his designer, Karl-Ernst Herrmann, used a huge film sound stage, filling it with a couple of trees, some other minor scenic elements, ramps, bench seating, music, sound effects and actors moving through the place, performing not only the words and actions of the play but a variety of other seemingly random activities. His staging of the play, in other words, was the enactment, within a created 'environment' shared by actors and audience, of a series of theatrical events provoked by the text – including both those described in the text and others suggested by it. Stein's response to the play when he began work on the production may remind some readers of their own feelings as they first encounter it. The play seemed to him 'totally foreign . . . so full of ideas, so complex and so lacking in consistency' that he found it hard to come to terms with. His production made no attempt to 'explain' *As You Like It*, only to create an experience of the play, including its curious inconsistencies, from the inside.

This handbook is meant to accompany the reader on her/his own journey through the play, first surveying the surroundings, then moving into the interior of the text, exploring the extraordinary, diverse imaginative space where it lives and discovering that the play's world isn't the faraway, 'magical' Forest of Arden at all, but a more ordinary place full of much greater wonders: a theatre.

My thanks to my students in the Staging Shakespeare MFA programme at Exeter University, to Professor John Russell Brown for his patience, and to Professor Donald Soule for his helpful advice.

L.W.S.

1 *The Text and Early Performances*

The text

The text of *As You Like It* is one of the least problematic of Shakespeare's works. There is only one original text, found in the First Folio of 1623, where it is the tenth of the thirty-six plays included. The earliest reference to the play is found in an entry in the Stationer's Register of 4 August 1600, in a list of plays 'to be staied':

> As you lyke it / a booke
> Henry the Ffift / a booke
> Euery man in his humour / a booke
> The Commedie of muche A doo about nothing. a booke.

Registering a play as 'to be staied' was often a means of forestalling the circulation of a pirated version, and is thus essentially a declaration of copyright. It was a common problem for the players' companies that an especially well-attended play would be transcribed from a live performance and printed without permission to capitalize on its current popularity. There is no concrete evidence, however, that *As You Like It* was drawing large audiences, as *Henry V* and *Every Man in His Humour* were. In fact, nothing is known about the play's popularity in its own time, aside from a suggestion (based on very speculative evidence unearthed in the nineteenth century) that it may have had a revival in 1603 (see Latham, 1975, pp. ix–x).

The copy of *As You Like It* from which the Folio version was printed seems to have been a good one. No one has suggested that it is anything but a reliable text deriving from Shakespeare's own draft or 'foul papers' [working copies]. All the evidence indicates that the

Folio text was printed from a transcript by a playhouse scribe, a fair copy of the prompt-book intended for indefinite future publication. This copy was probably made about 1600, when the play was first being performed on the stage.

It was an orderly manuscript, neatly divided into Acts and scenes, and generally more carefully prepared than the usual prompt copy. The indications of the speakers of lines are remarkably consistent, compared with most texts of the time, and some care is taken in the designation of characters: e.g., 'Duke Senior' is distinguished from 'Duke' (Frederick). There are very few stage directions, and then only the briefest possible: 'Flourish' (I.ii.138), 'Wrestle' (I.ii.200) or 'Music. Song' (IV.ii.10). There are also some costume indications (e.g., 'Enter Rosalind for Ganymede, Celia for Athena, Clown alias Touchstone', 'Duke Senior and lords, like outlaws'). It is a succinct, practically useful version of the play, rather than a literary presentation.

First performances

The first recorded performance of *As You Like It* is not until 1740, though several excerpts from the play had appeared in a pastiche called *Love in a Forest*, performed in 1723. The original performances of the play, however, occurred 140 years earlier, probably in 1599 – that is, later than a list of current plays issued in 1598 and before the 1600 Stationer's Register entry. The specific date of the first performance is unknown, though there are various factors which allow an intelligent guess to be made. The uncertainty is partly connected to the staying order. While the other three plays listed with it were all printed within twelve months, *As You Like It* was not. The reasons that may have lain behind this also tell us something about the possible date of the first performance.

The most notable of these derives from an edict issued on 1 June 1599 by the Archbishop of Canterbury and the Bishop of London prohibiting the printing of satires or epigrams unless they were approved by the appropriate authority, i.e., those appointed by the bishops as 'correctors'. This could have affected the printing of *As You Like It*, for the figure of the melancholy Jaques might have been taken as a satirical reference to Sir John Harington (see below, p. 7), a controversial figure linked to the Earl of Essex, who had recently fallen out of favour with the Queen and been taken into custody in September of 1599. Harington had already been in trouble with the monarch in 1596, with the publication of his *The Metamorphosis of Ajax*. This was a satirical discourse on his recent invention, the water closet, which had earned him the nickname 'Ajax', a pun on 'jakes' or 'jaques', an Elizabethan word for lavatory. Far-fetched as it may seem to us now, it is possible that one of the 'correctors' may have decided that Shakespeare's satirically portrayed Jaques was named after Harington's 'Ajax' and thus represented an indirect allusion to Essex. If this was the case, it was considered ample reason for not printing the play. It also provides a basis for supposing it may have been written and first performed in 1599 or 1600.

Other considerations increase the likelihood of this date. In 1598, two plays about Robin Hood were enjoying great success at the Rose Theatre (see the reference to this figure in I.ii.114–16). Another element is the popularity at this same time of pastoral romances and plays by John Lyly and others – a popularity *As You Like It* may have been intended to capitalize on.

There have been speculations, however, that there might have been a previous performance of the play in early 1599 (Shrovetide) for Queen Elizabeth at Richmond Palace. The suggestion arises out of the discovery of another epilogue, addressed to the Queen, which might have been written for *As You Like It*. The link with the play involves the presence in the courtyard of the Palace of a famous sundial and the prominent mention in the newly discovered epilogue of a dial, which in turn has suggested a possible connection to Jaques's mention of Touchstone's 'dial' (II.vii.20–3) and the several other mentions of time-keeping in the play (see Dusinberre, 2003, pp. 371–405).

Whatever the exact date of the play's composition and first performance, it seems quite certain that its first public performance was by Shakespeare's company, the Chamberlain's Men, in association with the opening of the new Globe Theatre some time in 1599. *As You Like It* would surely have been the sort of offering the company might think attractive for the occasion of opening a new public theatre.

Elizabethan performance

Knowing something about how *As You Like It* was first performed can clearly be important in reading it as a performance and staging it today. We are fortunate in this case that the theatre in which the play was first performed has been reconstructed as accurately as possible (though recent evidence suggests it may be slightly larger than the original). The new Globe Theatre in Southwark, a venue for frequent performances of Shakespeare's plays, provides us with a unique opportunity to learn about the conditions of Elizabethan public theatre performances, including the original *As You Like It*, and what can happen on the stage and between performers and audience when Elizabethan texts are played in such a theatre.

The most important architectural characteristic of the original Globe Theatre was the openness of stage and audience spaces to each other: players and audience shared a common space, without the separation commonly found in today's proscenium arch staging. One important consequence of the design of the stage area was the fluidity of actor movement it offered (indeed demanded) – a fluidity clearly called for by the *As You Like It* text. Most scenes were certainly played with considerable movement around the stage. Given that the performers were surrounded by spectators on three sides, it is also certain that they had to perpetually alter the direction in which they faced, in order to maintain contact (even eye contact) with spectators on all sides (as well as above them in the galleries). The result would have been a distinct tendency towards a circularity of movement, lending the performers something of the quality of dancers in a choreographed composition of performative interplay.

The theatre was also a large one, holding nearly 3000 spectators. The stage was approximately 40 feet wide, 25 feet deep and 5 feet high, and projected into the middle of the yard, which was about 80 feet in diameter and enclosed by three levels of galleries. (The modern reconstruction in Southwark has the same dimensions.) The original theatre confronted the players of *As You Like It* with a huge performance space, demanding considerable vocal skill and power and requiring movement and gesture on a large scale. It is interesting to note how the demands for a big performance would also probably have affected the delivery of different kinds and lengths of speeches by the actor. It is likely that short exchanges of dialogue could be directed to the other actors, with occasional visible reference to the audience, but particularly when it came to longer speeches (for example, more than 10–15 lines or about half a minute), performers would have had to perform, not with self-contained, introspective expressiveness, but openly to the large space around them – that is, to the audience. Even a soliloquy, in such conditions, becomes of necessity a kind of oration.

All in all, the arrangement of the theatre – together with the popular performance traditions from which it derived – evoked a strongly performative style of acting quite different from today's illusionistic realism. Such a style is also evidenced in the structuring of the texts, and especially in the modes of characterization. A character in the Elizabethan theatre was at least as much a stage role as a fictional person. Spectators were aware throughout of the presence of the performer, who was commonly called not 'actor' but 'player'. In particular, this meant that a character was performed more directly to the audience than we are accustomed to today, and this often included explicit direct address of the audience. The constant awareness of both players and spectators that they were participating in a theatrical performance meant that metatheatre was prevalent, particularly in comedies like *As You Like It*.

This style of performing, deriving from a long and lively tradition of popular performance at fairs and innyards, was free and physical, utilizing not only direct audience address but a variety of physical skills. No player worth his salt would have been deficient in singing, swordfighting or dancing. In addition, there were two kinds of specialist players whose influence on acting in general was undoubtedly great: the clown and the boy player. The clown was above all a popular performer and remained that, even when put in a play and given a fictional identity and name. In *As You Like It*, Touchstone provides a perpetual reminder of the clown's mixed functions. Similarly, the boy players who performed all women's roles were intrinsically metatheatrical by virtue of their youth and gender – possibly too because of the particular liveliness of their playing style, especially in comedy. The presence of the boy within/beside the female character was always apparent to spectators, even when they chose partially to suspend their disbelief, and therefore became a significant element in their perception and understanding of both play and performance.

Knowing something about the conditions of the first performance of *As You Like It* on the stage of the Globe Theatre in 1599 provides us with important information for reading the play. While there is little to be gained from merely attempting to replicate that performance (even if we could), trying to imagine its particulars as far as possible remains one valuable point of departure for imagining the play in performance.

2 *Cultural Contexts and Sources*

Conditions

The 1590s in England were a time of great activity in every area of public life. Elizabeth I had ruled since 1558. Born in 1533, she was growing old, but her subtlety and political skill were greater than ever and her grip on power remained secure. She continued to manipulate rival courtiers and, more importantly, the conflicting forces of English society. Her encouragement of buccaneer entrepreneurs like Francis Drake (together with good luck with the weather) had made possible the destruction of Spain's Armada in 1588 and the diminution of the perpetual Spanish naval and mercantile threat. Through long and delicate manoeuvrings to hold royal Continental suitors at bay, she had maintained her famous 'virginity', thus managing to sustain not only her personal independence, but that of England against traditional European rivals. Her policies stimulated the growth of entrepreneurial trade, which had already led to the exploration and exploitation of the new world and of the East, such as Walter Ralegh's discovery and annexation of Virginia in 1584 and, the year before, voyages by the merchants Ralph Fitch and John Eldred to India and the Persian Gulf. The expansion of global trade ventures was accompanied by a comparable growth of the internal economy, with the power of a newly rich merchant class starting to rival that of the traditional aristocracy. At the same time, by refusing to name an heir, Elizabeth created persistent tensions within her court, as rival lords strove to further the claims of various aspirants to the throne. Court and national politics were a dangerous game, the consequences of which could extend even into the field of theatre, as the business of Sir John Harington and Essex makes clear.

The 1590s were a time of more than political turmoil: the landscape of English culture was also changing rapidly. In the course of the century, the religious preoccupations of the Middle Ages had been overtaken – though hardly erased – by the rise of humanism. The Elizabethan was above all an age when the individual human being in all her/his perceived splendour and diversity was perceived as central. A significant sign of this was the rapidly growing interest in drama and, more and more as the century drew to a close, in the representation of varied individuals, of which the gallery of characters in *As You Like It* is a good example. The age's interest in 'character' was both literary and scientific. The former had carried over from classical times and Plutarch's *Lives* and the *Characters* of Theophrastus (which appeared in a new Latin translation in 1592) were much read at the time, and in the first decade of the new century Joseph Hall and Sir Thomas Overbury published new books of 'characters', collections of brief sketches of well-known personality and occupational types. A 'scientific' perception of characters as defined by the distribution of 'humours' became current, most famously in Jonson's *Every Man in His Humour* (1598). A particularly popular character type was the melancholic, of which Jaques is a classic example. The growth of medical science also included an interest in melancholy as a psychological phenomenon. A prime example of this approach is Timothy Bright's *A Treatise of Melancholie* (1586), a work Shakespeare is thought to have read. Bright explores the difference between 'natural' melancholy and that deriving from guilt feelings, or an 'afflicted conscience'. Though Jaques's melancholy seems mostly an adopted pose, that it may have a moral dimension is suggested by Duke Senior's sharp comments on his sinful past as a 'libertine' (II.vii.64–9).

Another area of significant change in the period was the countryside, commonly referred to as 'forest', a legal term designating more than just woods. 'A Treatise . . . of the Laws of the Forest', an edition of which appeared in 1598, defines a 'forest' as 'certain territory of woody grounds and fruitful pastures' (quoted in Hattaway, 2000, p. 3, n. 2), that is, both wild forest and working farmland. For this reason, the 'forests' of plays like Peele's popular *Old Wives' Tale* (published 1595) often included both farcical country bumpkins and magical sylvan spirits in almost equal measure, just as the Forest of

Arden in *As You Like It* contains both the sheep and goats of Corin and Audrey and the sylvan retreat of Duke Senior and his court.

Far from being perpetually bountiful, England's 'fruitful pastures' were subject to frequent plagues and bad harvests. In addition to these threats, the development of a rich mercantile class in the city was paralleled by the rise of profit-seeking landowners evicting and buying out smaller landowners. The pressure towards profitability meant a substantial increase in sheep-raising for the production of both wool and manure for farming. More and more, the seizure of common land for the purposes of sheep-grazing had dire consequences for many country people, and was the cause of discontent and even riots. The increase in absentee landlords like Corin's master (II.iv.76–84), in effect turned peasants into waged labourers, who could be discharged at will. Even when not absentee, these same landowners often sought to improve their social status by an increased reliance on primogeniture as a way of consolidating property and achieving gentlemanly status. John Stephens, in his *Essays and Characters* (1615), writes of the typical farmer, who 'murmurs against the Tribune's law, by which none might occupy more than five hundred acres . . . because he cannot purchase more' and for whom 'the bringing up and marriage of his eldest son is an ambition which afflicts him', as well as 'the hope to see his son superior, or placed above him' (Wilson, 1926, p. 12). As a consequence of these developments, more and more younger sons like Orlando were thrust out into the world to make their own way. A further result was the breakdown of the traditional household, based on the old forms of dependence: 'the constant service of the antique world' (II.iii.57). Long-serving retainers like Adam were often disposed of as uneconomical, a practice much decried by writers such as Gervase Markham.

An important aspect of the 'woody grounds' or sylvan part of the forest was its function as the site of deer-hunting, the traditional sport of monarchs and the landed aristocracy and still generally regarded as the noblest of sports. 'The hunting of wild beasts in general' was described by Gervase Markham, writing in 1611, as of all recreations the 'most royal for the stateliness thereof, most artificial [artful] for the wisdom and cunning thereof, and most manly for the use and endurance thereof' (Wilson, 1926, p. 16). Hunting is mentioned in Lodge's *Rosalynde* (see, for example, Bullough, 1963, vol. 2, p. 200) and of course several times in *As You Like It*. In both cases, it is presented as an appropriate forest sport for gentlemen, who were none the less reviled by the yeomanry for enclosing useful pasturage or farming land as private preserves for their sport. As a general rule, however, the countryside – both rural and sylvan – is not represented in the literature of the time as part of the real world, but as a world of escape, to which characters go to 'find themselves' in a time of revels, through which they achieve freedom from the strictures of the city and court.

In part, *As You Like It* is representative of this treatment. The realities of country and village life find their way into the play in several ways, however, as evidenced in the play's festive structure and in characters like Corin and Audrey (see below, Chapter 3, *passim*, and Chapter 6, p. 159). Also to be seen are the prevalent Elizabethan assumptions about political authority, class and gender, for example, in the two Dukes, the relations between court and country characters, and the interaction of Rosalind with Orlando and others (see below, Chapter 3, *passim*, and Chapter 6, pp. 159, 160–1).

While English society had become significantly secularized in the course of the century, the controversy between the old Church of Rome and the new Protestantism continued. By the 1590s, the conflict between the now firmly established English church and the rising forces of puritanism (with Catholicism continuing to be a dangerous undercurrent) also became a major source of tension in political and cultural life. In London, the Puritanically inclined Mayor and aldermen had been hostile to theatrical companies and performances ever since they had begun to rise in popularity in the third quarter of the century. Theatrical companies, each under the patronage of a powerful nobleman, had grown rapidly and, as the century drew to a close, were enjoying considerable success. But there continued to be a strong current of disapproval of theatrical performance.

In 1597, the officers of the Guildhall petitioned the Queen and her Privy Council to suppress all 'stage plays at the Theatre, Curtain and Bankside as in all other places in and about the City'. If the Court were to remove its support, stage players, who as an itinerant class had always depended on the tolerance and patronage of the land-owning aristocracy, would effectively become vagrants, subject to the 1572 Act 'for the punishment of Vagabonds and for Relief of the Poor and Impotent'. Responding to the Guildhall's complaint, the Privy Council issued an order that threatened to spell the end of professional theatre in England:

> Her Majesty being informed that there are very great disorders committed in the common playhouses both by lewd matters that are handled on the stages and by resort and confluence of bad people, hath given direction that not only no plays shall be used within London or about the city or in any public place during this time of summer, but also those playhouses that are erected and built only for such purposes shall be plucked down. (Wickham et al., 2000, p. 100)

That this order did not actually result in existing theatres being closed and 'plucked down' was probably due not only to the wide popularity of theatrical performance, but perhaps even more to the patronage of powerful noblemen (not to mention the Queen's known fondness for theatrical performances at Court). It is no accident that in 1599 the two leading companies, the Lord Admiral's Men at the Rose Theatre and the Lord Chamberlain's Men at Burbage's Theatre and then the newly opened Globe, had as their patrons noblemen who were members of the Queen's Privy Council. In consequence, these companies were relatively, though never entirely, safe from Guildhall interference.

In a period of enormous vitality and change, however, and in a city whose population doubled between 1580 and 1600 from 100,000 to 200,000 (out of a total of only 4,000,000 in all of England – Gurr, 1987, p. 50), such constraints could not have stopped the growing demand for more theatre. By the end of the century, London's burgeoning and varied population had developed a hearty appetite for plays and the public theatres were generally filled nearly every afternoon for most of the year.

There can be little doubt that in Elizabethan public theatre performances the occasion was dominated by the presence of the audience. The Globe Theatre, for example, held up to 3000 spectators (estimates vary), with more than 800 in the yard and another 1500 in the three galleries: a huge crowd for such an enclosed space. A theatrical performance in these conditions was more like a carnival gathering than a modern theatre performance, for Elizabethans were not the well-behaved theatrical spectators of today. At least until their interest was caught and held, they were an active, noisy lot. Spectators' conduct may be best understood as, to a considerable degree, an extension of street behaviour. The close proximity of bodies encouraged all the jostling, shifting, nudging and elbowing one would find in a crowded market, as well as free exchanges of greetings and jibes, and ribald comments on the performance.

Despite the widespread illiteracy of the time, London had an exceptionally large number of literate workers – many unemployed, with time to go to the theatre – and the greatest concentration of rich citizenry and gentry in the country. It is therefore very likely that public theatre audiences had 'a similarly exceptional level of literacy, wealth and poverty' (Gurr, 1987, p. 55). There was a mixture of occupations and ages, and both sexes were represented (though men predominated). Edmund Spenser, writing in 1596, describes the 'troublous noise' of 'women's cries and the shouts of boys' (Spenser, 1978, p. 602), and it is clear that there was a considerable number of young artisans, apprentices and unhoused casual workers standing in the yard, and women of repute and disrepute scattered throughout the theatre. Despite their higher proportion of literacy than among the general population, a large number of spectators, including most of the women, were probably substantially illiterate. To make up for it, however, Elizabethan spectators were good listeners, practised in listening to sermons and often attending the law courts for recreation.

They were also good talkers – and therefore vociferous spectators. Audience response could frequently include comments called out to the actors, 'Shouts and Claps at ev'ry little pause' (Gurr, 1987, p. 215), as well as humming and hawking. Hissing and laughing and stamping or knocking were also common responses to the performance. Such participation was not only endured by the actors, but encouraged, especially in comedies. The satirical essay 'A Common Player' (1611) describes a frequent practice: 'When he doth hold conference [with another player] on the stage; and should look directly in his fellow's face; he turns about his voice into the assembly for applause-sake, like a trumpeter in the fields, that shifts places to get an echo' (quoted in Gurr, 1987, p. 228). (The description might well have applied particularly to the player of Touchstone.) The play's text was of course clearly spoken, but undoubtedly supplemented by the performers' own additions and elaborations, frequently addressed directly to the audience. M. C. Bradbrook has described some of the kinds of stage–audience interaction that occurred:

> Appeals to the audience, soliloquies and asides directed towards them, and sudden allusions to familiar scenes or everyday events . . . would be varied according to the nature of the listeners. Actors might turn towards the principal spectator, might interpolate a few words or reword a scene. . . . Insistent calls for the clown might bring him on.   (Bradbrook, 1955, p. 14)

Spectators came not just expecting to become engaged in the illusory lives of dramatic characters, but inclined at the same time to carry on a lively theatrical interplay with the performers.

Performances were offered by a variety of theatrical companies, associations of share-holding actors and others, who gathered the resources to stage as many plays as there were audiences for. In 1599, the leading companies were the Lord Admiral's Men and Shakespeare's company, the Lord Chamberlain's Men. The shareholders of the companies financed productions and divided the profits proportionately. The theatre's owner had to be paid for the use of the building (normally half the gallery receipts) and there were many other expenses, notably the weekly wages of the actors, musicians, wardrobe master (tire-man), prompter (book-keeper) and stage hands. The boys who played all the female roles were for the most part apprenticed to company members, who fed and lodged them. These youths often grew into adult actors, though the exploitation they suffered as boys means that, with few exceptions, their names are unknown to us. But they were important members of the company and many established considerable reputations. The anonymous boy who played Rosalind would have been one of the best of them. He must already have become a very highly regarded professional to be entrusted with the key role in a new play intended for performance at the opening of an important new theatre.

Particularly popular members of the acting companies were the clowns. As a type, they had survived for centuries in various kinds of performances, including mummers' plays, fairs and carnivals. In the plays of the early Elizabethan period, the clown function was often performed by the Vice, a ribald, undisciplined player who usually functioned quite independently of the play's fictional action and in frequent direct contact with the spectators. This tradition of free play by clowns continued at least till the end of the century. As Jonathan Holmes observes, 'the signifier "clown" refers to a type of role, rather than a coherent character . . . a type with a known player: either Will Kempe or Robert Armin' (Holmes, 2004, p. 25). The most memorable clown in the last decades of the sixteenth century was Dick Tarlton, who was extremely popular throughout the 1570s and 1580s. His style was rumbustious and noisy, involving much physical knock-about, sharp wit and aggressive vulgarity. He was an unpredictable performer, whose entrances were famous: 'The people began exceedingly to laugh when Tarlton first peeped out his head' from behind the stage curtain, writes one contemporary (Nashe, 1904, vol. 1, p. 188). He also liked to engage in aggressive backchat with the audience, often singling out one spectator, whom he proceeded to ridicule and humiliate, to the great amusement of the crowd.

By the 1590s, Tarlton's time had passed (he died in 1588) and he was succeeded by somewhat less aggressive and independent clowns, notably Will Kempe and Robert Armin, who were consecutive members of Shakespeare's company. Kempe's speciality seems to have been a ludicrous country bumpkin character (such as William in *As You Like It*, though he did not play the role). He was also famous for his jigs, the song and dance afterpieces, dominated by the clowns, commonly staged (until about the end of the century) at the end of plays. Kempe was a member of the Chamberlain's Men, but left the company at the time that they opened the new Globe Theatre, perhaps owing to some disagreement with his fellows. His place was taken by Robert Armin, said to be Dick Tarlton's choice as his successor, but quite a different kind of clown from the more old-fashioned

Kempe. He was certainly a versatile performer, capable, in his own words, of playing

> A flat fool and a fat fool,
> A lean fool and a clean fool,
> A merry fool and a very fool.
>> (quoted in Holmes, 2004, p. 26)

That Armin played Touchstone seems certain, for he was known to have been a goldsmith before turning to the stage and had written and played a character called 'Tutch' in several popular entertainments. That Armin performed the role is made even likelier by the fact that William, the country clown, appears to be an intentional reference to the departed Will Kempe: the name 'William' is repeated four times in his one short scene (V.i.14, 20–1, 58). There is reason to think that Shakespeare may also have written the part of Amiens for Armin, who was known to be an excellent singer. Since Touchstone and Amiens never appear at the same time (except for the last scene, where Amiens is credited with entering, but has no lines), the two parts could easily have been doubled, a common practice at the time.

Influences

A great variety of dramatic types appeared on the public and private stages from the 1580s onwards, as the early plays of Shakespeare himself make clear. Of the twenty plays conventionally assigned to the 1590s, seven are comedies, nine are historical and the remaining four either tragedy or tragi-comedy (if *Titus Andronicus* and *The Merchant of Venice* may be so called). Historical subjects were popular in the period, but their purpose (as plays such as *Julius Caesar* or *Richard III* make particularly clear) was by no means primarily what today would be called historical. Comedy was, as always, a dominant genre, but it came in many and mixed forms. Widely different styles and subject matter often occurred in a single play. Highly stylized romantic material was commonly mixed with simple, earthy language and with characters and scenes clearly belonging to popular farce (see the excerpt from *Mucedorus* below). The result was loosely structured hybrids. Lyly, in his 1590 prologue to *Midas*, acknowledged this phenomenon: 'What heretofore hath been served in several dishes for a feast, is now minced in a charger for a gallimaufry. If we present a mingle-mangle, our fault is to be excused, because the whole world is become a Hodge-Podge' (Lyly, 1988, p. 201). The majority of plays presented in the public theatres defied categorization, dealing with a wide range of subjects, backgrounds and character types. This melange of plays was an important part of the theatrical and literary context in which Shakespeare created *As You Like It*.

A significant component of that context was the pastoral. While partly expressing the traditional interest in the countryside, the pastoral was essentially an extension of the romance, deriving largely from classical and Renaissance Italian sources. Prominent among Elizabethan pastoral works was Edmund Spenser's *The Shephearde's Calendar* (1579), a collection of eclogues (poetic dialogues among shepherds) modelled on those of Theocritus and Virgil. Another important contribution to the genre was Philip Sidney's *Arcadia*, first published in 1593 and maintaining its popularity through the nineties and beyond. Ariosto's *Orlando Furioso* (1532) was a particularly influential pastoral romance. It was translated by Sir John Harington in 1591 and adapted as a play in the same year by Robert Greene. Its setting is not unlike *As You Like It*'s Forest of Arden. Here too the trees of the forest are hung with 'roundelays', though in this case they have been written not by the hero but by his rival, in hopes of arousing his jealousy. While interesting, such parallels are not as significant as they might appear, however, for such devices were commonplaces of the pastoral form.

Related in style and tone to the pastoral, the romance (of which Lodge's *Rosalynde* is an example) was another influential type of the period. Among the more successful examples of adaptations of romances into drama are those of John Lyly. Before turning to playwriting, Lyly enjoyed his first success with a prose work, *Euphues, the Anatomy of Wit* (1578). A witty romance, whose content is very like a morality play, it was renowned for its innovative prose style, which came to be known as Euphuism and exerted considerable influence in the following decades. It is a highly mannered style, involving the use of carefully balanced antitheses and parallel sentence structures, as well as clever repetition, assonance and alliteration (all of which can be found in abundance in *As You Like It*, as in its primary source, *Rosalynde*). A few years after *Euphues*, Lyly had further success with his plays, classically derived and wittily stylized comedies written for performance by boys' companies, most notably the Boys of St Paul's at Elizabeth's court, where they were received with enthusiasm. These plays Shakespeare would surely have read, and traces of their likely influence can be seen in his comedies.

Lyly's *Gallathea*, performed at Court in 1588 and printed in 1592, may well have had some effect upon certain elements of *As You Like It*. The scholarly consensus is that Shakespeare almost certainly knew *Gallathea*, and that the equivocal scenes between Gallathea and Phillida might have been in his mind as he depicted Rosalind and Orlando's whimsical wooing. All the roles in Lyly's play were acted by schoolboys, whose playful manner is evident in the easy wit and light-hearted formality (echoed in the style of Rosalind and Celia), which would have been enjoyed by the aristocratic audience. The relationship and dialogue between Lyly's two young women (disguised as boys by their fathers to escape possible sacrifice to a sea-monster) contain hints of the kind of subtextual nuances Shakespeare later introduced into Ganymede's scenes with Orlando and, particularly, with Phebe. The following excerpts give a suggestion:

Enter PHILLIDA *and* GALLATHEA

PHILLIDA   It is a pity nature framed you not a woman, having a face so fair, so lovely a countenance, so modest a behaviour. . . . I say it is a pity you are not a woman.

GALLATHEA   I would not wish to be a woman, unless it were because thou art a man.

PHILLIDA   Nay, I do not wish to be a woman, for then I should not love thee. For I have sworn never to love a woman.

GALLATHEA   A strange humour in so pretty a youth, and according to mine, for myself will never love a woman. . . .

After much clever equivocation, the question of gender continues to preoccupy the characters.

PHILLIDA [*aside*]   What doubtful speeches be these? I fear me he is as I am,
   a maiden.
GALLATHEA [*aside*]   What dread riseth in my mind? I fear the boy to be as
   I am, a maiden.
PHILLIDA [aside]   Tush, it cannot be. His voice shows the contrary.
GALLATHEA [aside]   Yet I do not think it, for he would then have blushed.
   . . .

(Act III, scene ii, Daniel, 1988, pp. 125–6)

When the threat of sacrifice is over, their fathers return, together
with Neptune, Diana and Venus. Learning each other's true identities,
the girls, now distraught, are offered an interesting solution by
Venus:

NEPTUNE   Do you both, being maidens, love one another?
GALLATHEA   I had thought the habit agreeable with the sex, and so
   burned in the fire of my own fancies.
PHILLIDA   I had thought that in the attire of a boy, there could not have
   lodged the body of a virgin, and so was inflamed with a sweet desire,
   which now I find a sour deceit.
DIANA   Now things falling out as they do, you must leave these fond,
   fond affections. Nature will have it so; necessity must.
GALLATHEA   I will never love any but Phillida. Her love is engraven in my
   heart with her eyes.
PHILLIDA   Nor I any but Gallathea, whose faith is imprinted in my
   thoughts by her words.
NEPTUNE   An idle choice, strange and foolish, for one virgin to dote on
   another and to imagine a constant faith where there can be no cause
   of affection. How like you this,Venus?
VENUS   I like well and allow it. They shall both be possessed of their
   wishes, for never shall it be said that nature or fortune shall overthrow
   love and faith. Is your love unspotted, begun with truth, continued
   with constancy, and not to be altered till death?
GALLATHEA   Die, Gallathea, if thy love be not so.
PHILLIDA   Accursed be thou, Phillida, if they love be not so.
DIANA   Suppose all this, Venus. What then?
VENUS   Then shall it be seen that I can turn one of them to be a man, and
   that I will. . . . Then let us depart. Neither of them shall know whose
   lot it shall be till they come to the church door. One shall be. Doth it
   suffice?

PHILLIDA   And satisfy us both, doth it not, Gallathea?
GALLATHEA   Yes, Phillida.

> [*Exeunt all but* GALLATHEA]
> (Act V, scene iii, Daniel, 1988, pp. 140–2)

Other plays of the 1580s and 1990s were clearer examples of Lyly's 'mingle-mangle', particularly those played in the public theatres. Their looseness of structure and content help to explain the variety of styles found in *As You Like It*. A popular and typical example of such theatrical *bricolage* was Robert Greene's *Friar Bacon and Friar Bungay* (*c.* 1589), a free-wheeling treatment of the story of two thirteenth-century 'magicians' who were Franciscan friars. The wide range of the dramatic personae – from King Henry the Third to Joan, 'a country wench' – suggests something of the play's loose and whimsical style, and recalls Sidney's condemnation in his *Apology for Poetry* of plays in which clowns and kings were too freely mixed.

Another lively example of the freedom with which disparate elements were mingled in the 1590s is the anonymous *Mucedorus*. The play was first printed in 1598, though it had undoubtedly often been played earlier, and was reprinted and performed for many years thereafter. The main story is derived from Sidney's popular and sophisticated romance *Arcadia*, but the treatment of the material is rough and ready, and the romance is mixed with many other elements, including a clown called Mouse and a wild man of the forest (a figure from folk tales). A suggestion of the flavour of this sort of popular 'mingle-mangle' may be got from the following brief extract, with its mixture of lofty sentiment and farcical brutality. At the same time, it helps us to appreciate how very differently Shakespeare dealt with roughly similar fictional material.

The hero, a prince disguised as a shepherd, rescues his lady from a bear. Later, as she again takes refuge in the forest, this time to avoid having to marry the man her father has given her to, she is taken prisoner by Bremo, the wild man, from whom she saves the hero, by now in a new disguise as a hermit. He is also captured and enslaved by the wild man and the two lovers meet again as their captor briefly leaves them alone together:

MUCEDORUS   Pardon my boldness, fair lady; sith we both
     May safely talk now out of Bremo's sight,
     Unfold to me, if you so please, the full discourse
     How, when, and why you came into these woods,
     And fell into this bloody butcher's hands.
AMADINE   Hermit, I will.
     Of late a worthy shepherd I did love –
MUCEDORUS   A shepherd, lady? Sure, a man unfit
     To match with you.
AMADINE   Hermit, this is true; and when we had –
MUCEDORUS   Stay there; the wild man comes!
     Refer the rest until another time.

With the return of Bremo the wild man, the two lovers pretend to be afraid in the forest and ask him to teach them how to protect themselves. He agrees, fashions a 'knotty crabtree staff' and offers it to Mucedorus to learn how to use it:

BREMO   Then take my staff and see how thou canst wield it.
MUCEDORUS   First teach me how to hold it in my hand.
BREMO   Thou holdst it well.
     Look how he doth; thou mayst the sooner learn.
MUCEDORUS   Next tell me how and when 'tis best to strike.
BREMO   'Tis best to strike when time doth serve;
     'Tis best to lose no time.
MUCEDORUS [*Aside*]   Then now or never is my time to strike.
BREMO   And, when thou strikest, be sure to hit the head.
MUCEDORUS   The head?
BREMO   The very head.
MUCEDORUS   Then have at thine!
     He strikes him down dead.
     So lie there and die,
     A death no doubt according to desert,
     Or else a worse as thou deservst a worse.
AMADINE   It glads my heart this tyrant's death to see.
MUCEDORUS   Now, lady, it remains in you
     To end the tale you lately had begun,
     Being interrupted by this wicked wight.
     You said you loved a shepherd?
AMADINE   Ay, so I do, and none but only him.

And will do still as long as life shall last.

MUCEDORUS   But tell me, lady, sith I set you free,
   What course of life do you intend to take?

AMADINE   I will disguisèd wander through the world,
   Till I have found him out.

MUCEDORUS   How if you find your shepherd in these woods?

ADAMINE   Ah, none so happy then as Amadine.
     He discloseth himself.

MUCEDORUS   In tract of time a man may alter much.
   Say, lady, do you know your shepherd well?

AMADINE   My Mucedorus! Hath he set me free?

MUCEDORUS   He hath set thee free.

AMADINE   And lived so long unknown to Amadine?

MUCEDORUS   Ay, that's a question whereof you may not be resolved.
   You know that I am banished from the court?
   I know likewise each passage is beset
   So that we cannot long escape unknown;
   Therefore my will is this: that we return
   Right through the thickets to the wild man's cave,
   And there awhile live on his provision,
   Until the search and narrow watch be past.
   This is my counsel, and I think it best.

AMADINE   I think the very same.

MUCEDORUS   Come, let's begone.

They go out and more farcical business ensues:

> *The Clown [enters and] searcheth, and falls over the Wild Man,*
> *and so carries him away.*
>> (*Mucedorus*, scene xvii, lines 23–98,
>> Baskervill et al., 1934, pp. 547–8)

Such scrambled romantic plays continued to be performed throughout the decade, but by its end public taste was beginning to change and another kind of comedy was becoming increasingly popular. This newer style, while often continuing the tradition of farce, involved a greater degree of realism. The lives of ordinary London people became a common subject, particularly in those plays belonging to the genre called 'citizen comedy', which depicted the day-to-day lives of London tradesmen. An outstanding example, written in the same year as *As You Like It*, is Thomas Dekker's *The Shoemaker's Holiday*. The play's leading character is a shoemaker, Simon Eyre, shown in the following excerpt starting a day's work in his Tower Street shop. (One present-day difficulty with such plays is that their language is often so topical and idiomatic that we now need footnotes to understand many of the words.)

Enter Eyre, making himself ready

EYRE   Where be these boys, these girls, these drabs, these scoundrels? They wallow in the fat brewis [broth] of my bounty, and lick up the crumbs of my table, yet will not rise to see my walks cleansed. Come out, you powder-beef [salted beef] queans! What, Nan! What, Madge Mumblecrust! Come out, you fat midriff-swag-belly-whores, and sweep me these kennels [gutters] that the noisome stench offend not the nose of my neighbours. What, Firk, I say! What, Hodge! Open my shop windows! What, Firk, I say!

Enter Firk

FIRK   O master, is't you that speak bandog and bedlam [watchdog and madman] this morning? I was in a dream and mused what madman was got into the street so early. Have you drunk this morning that your throat is so clear?

EYRE   Oh, well said, Firk; well said, Firk. To work, my fine knave, to work! Wash thy face, and thou't be more blessed.

FIRK   Let them wash my face that will eat it. Good master, send for a souse-wife [a pig-pickler] if you'll have my face cleaner. . . .

EYRE   Away, sloven! Avaunt, scoundrel! . . .

Enter Eyre's Wife

EYRE   How now, Dame Margery, can you see to rise? Trip and go; call up the drabs, your maids.

WIFE   See to rise? I hope 'tis time enough; 'tis early enough for any woman to be seen abroad. I marvel how many wives of Tower Street are up so soon. God's me, 'tis not noon! Here's a yawling!

EYRE   Peace, Margery, peace! Where's Cisly Bumtrinket, your maid? She has a privy fault – she farts in her sleep. Call the quean up!

(Scene iv, Baskervill et al., 1934, p. 562)

The playwrights of the time were influenced not only by popular theatrical practices, but by literary tradition and the artistic currents of the age. Many of the influential dramatists of the 1580s had come out of the Universities, men such as the 'University Wits' Marlowe, Greene, Nashe and Peele, who often begrudged the popularity of 'upstart' newcomers like Shakespeare. Though Shakespeare himself knew 'little Latin and less Greek', both his dramatic and non-dramatic writing display an awareness of a variety of classical authors – though whether first- or second-hand we cannot know. In *As You Like It*, we detect the background presence of (as well as references to) such classical authors as Plutarch, Cicero, Tasso and, above all, Ovid. Orlando's speech in Act III, scene i, for example, echoes the tone and mythological characters of Ovid's *Metamorphoses*, a work that had proved a fruitful and suggestive source for the transformations and language of lovers in many dramatic and non-dramatic pastorals of the time. Earlier writers of the Italian Renaissance, such as Petrarch and Ariosto, also contributed to the romance tradition so strongly continued in Elizabethan verse and drama. Their influence on the pastoral writing of earlier Elizabethan writers, notably Edmund Spenser's *The Shephearde's Calendar* and *The Faerie Queene* and Sidney's *Arcadia*, was considerable.

Of course, when we refer to such a wide variety of writing as 'influences', we are using the word broadly. Whether it affected what Shakespeare wrote in any obvious and discernible way we can rarely know with any certainty, but this theatrical and literary world was the breeding ground for his plays. Thus, even plays such as *Mucedorus* and *The Shoemaker's Holiday*, though neither specific 'sources' nor discernible 'influences' on *As You Like It*, are pieces which illuminate the play by their very differences from it.

Sources

'Sources' usually means materials there is reason to believe may actually have suggested a play, or been used or adapted in writing it. They may be pieces of writing or real people or events; their effect may be direct or indirect, general or relevant only to particular parts of the play. Some sources are demonstrably evident, others only speculative possibilities. An example of the speculative is the suggestion that the character of Jaques may have been based on some contemporary

figure, the two favourite candidates being John Marston, as a model
of the satirist, and Sir John Harington (see above, p. 3), called 'the un-
licensed fool of Elizabeth's court' (Latham, 1975, p. xlviii). A more
general literary (though still speculative) source for the play, in
particular for its treatment of the main characters, may have been
Diana, a pastoral romance by the Portuguese author Jorge de
Montemayor, a translation of which was published in 1598. It has
been suggested that the tendency of some of Montemayor's lovers to
laugh at themselves may have influenced Shakespeare's characterization of Rosalind, though an ironic attitude towards their own affairs
of the heart is common in the heroines of romance. An even more
generalized influence on Shakespeare's handling of love in a pastoral
setting may have been Giovanni Battista Guarini's play *Il pastor fido*
(1590), in which the hero achieves his joy only through suffering,
somewhat as Orlando may be said to do.

A more specific possible source of *As You Like It* – in particular of
the story of Orlando and Oliver – was a medieval romance known as
The Tale of Gamelyn. It tells the story of the two sons of an old knight,
the elder of whom attempts to deprive his brother of his inheritance.
The eponymous hero, a younger son, enters a wrestling match and
unexpectedly triumphs. Subsequently tyrannized and threatened by
his older brother, he runs away with Adam the spencer [steward] and
joins a band of outlaws. His brother, now the sheriff, arrests him and
puts him in prison, but he is released through the unexpected inter-
vention of a third brother and returns to the forest. Ultimately he
returns, avenges himself on his eldest brother by hanging him, and
becomes Chief Justice of the royal forests.

Whether Shakespeare actually knew this tale cannot be known,
but it was certainly used by the author of the work which was unmistakably Shakespeare's main source for *As You Like It*: Thomas Lodge's
Rosalynde. The full title of this prose romance was *Rosalynde. Euphues
Golden Legacy. Found after his death in his Cell at Silexedra. Bequeathed to
Philautus sonnes, nursed-up with their Father in England*. The work first
appeared in 1590, though its popularity led to further printings in
1592, 1596, 1598 and later. Lodge, like Lyly, was a student at Oxford in
the 1570s, where from Latin examples they learned the witty,
balanced style made famous in *Euphues* by Lyly, to whom Lodge pays

tribute in his subtitle. *Rosalynde* is adapted partly from *The Tale of Gamelyn* and partly from Sidney and Robert Greene. Much of it is Lodge's own invention, however: notably the stories of Rosalynde and Alinda, who became Shakespeare's Rosalind and Celia.

Rosalynde is a very skilful piece of work, cleverly exploiting the current vogues for pastoral and euphuism. Being a prose narrative, the story is much more completely told than in Shakespeare's highly selective adaptation for the stage. The following summary, with excerpts, is helpful in seeing how Shakespeare made use of his source material. The relevant comparable passages in *As You Like It* are indicated in bold type.

Lodge's story is concerned with the fates of the three sons of Sir John of Bordeaux (Sir Rowland de Boys): Saladyne (Oliver), Fernandyne (Jaques de Boys) and Rosader (Orlando), who are left relatively equal portions in their father's will. Relying on the widely accepted tradition of primogeniture, the eldest brother decides to ignore the will's provisions and take the properties for himself. The second brother is encouraged to bury himself in his studies in Paris, while Saladyne determines that Rosader, his youngest brother, shall 'know little, so he shall not be able to execute much' (Bullough, 1963, vol. 2, p. 166. All the following page references are to this volume. The spellings have been modernized.)

> The young gentleman bore all with patience, till on a day walking in the garden by himself, he began to consider how he was the son of John of Bordeaux, a knight renowned for many victories, and a gentleman famous for his virtues, how contrary to the treatment of his father, he was not only kept from his land, and treated as a servant, but smothered in such secret slavery, as he might not attain to any honourable actions. Ay quoth he to himself (nature working these effectual passions) why should I that am a gentleman born, pass my time in such unnatural drudgery? Were it not better either in Paris to become a scholar, or in the court a courtier, or in the field a soldier, than to live a foot boy to my own brother: nature hath lent me wit to conceive, but my brother denied me art to contemplate: I have strength to perform any honourable exploit, but no liberty to accomplish my virtuous endeavours. These good parts that God hath bestowed upon me, the envy of my brother doth smother in obscurity: the harder is my fortune, and the more his forwardness.

With that casting up his hand he felt hair on his face, and perceiving his beard to bud, for choler he began to blush, and swore to himself he would be no more subject to such slavery. As thus he was ruminating his melancholy passions, in came Saladyne with his men, and seeing his brother in a brown study, and to forget his wonted reverence, thought to shake him out of his dumps thus. Sirrah (quoth he) what, is your heart on your half-penny, or are you saying a dirge for your father's soul? What, is my dinner ready? At this question Rosader turning his head askance, and bending his brows as if anger there had ploughed the furrows of her wrath, with his eyes full of fire, he made this reply. Dost thou ask me (Saladyne) for thy cates [food]? Ask some of thy churls who are fit for such an office. I am thy equal by nature, though not by birth, and though thou hast more cards in the bunch, I have as many trumps in my hands as thyself. Let me question with thee, why hast thou felled my Woods, spoiled my manor houses, and made havoc of such utensils as my father bequeathed unto me? I tell thee Saladyne, either answer me as a brother, or I will trouble thee as an enemy. At this reply of Rosader's, Saladyne smiled as laughing at his presumption, and frowned as checking his folly: he therefore took him up thus shortly. What sirrah, well I see pricks the tree that will prove a thorn. Hath my familiar conversing with you made you coy, or my good looks drawn you to be thus contemptuous? I can quickly remedy such a fault, and I will bend the tree while it is a wand. In faith (sir boy) I have a snaffle for such a headlong colt. You sirs, lay hold on him and bind him, and then I will give him a cooling card for his choler. This made Rosader half mad, that stepping to a great rake that stood in the garden, he laid such load on upon his brother's men that he hurt some of them, and made the rest of them run away. Saladyne seeing Rosader so resolute, and with his resolution so valiant, thought his heels his best safety, and took him to a loft adjoining to the garden, whither Rosader pursued him hotly. Saladyne afraid of his brother's fury, cried out to him thus. Rosader be not so rash, I am thy brother and thy elder, and if I have done thee wrong I'll make thee amends. Revenge not anger in blood, for so thou shalt stain the virtue of old Sir John of Bordeaux. Say wherein thou art discontent and thou shalt be satisfied. Brothers' frowns ought not to be periods of wrath. What man, look not so sourly, I know we shall be friends, and better friends than we have been. For, *Amantium irae amoris redintegratio est* [The quarrelling of lovers is the knitting up of love].

These words appeased the choler of Rosader (for he was of a mild and courteous nature) so that he laid down his weapons, and upon the faith of a gentleman assured his brother he would offer him no prejudice.

Whereupon Saladyne came down, and after a little parley they embraced each other and became friends, and Saladyne promising Rosader restitution of all his lands, and what favour else (quoth he) any ways my ability or the nature of a brother may perform. Upon these sugared reconciliations they went into the house arm in arm together, to the great content of all the old servants of Sir John of Bordeaux.   (pp. 166–8; **compare with *As You Like It*, I.i**)

Saladyne, however, plots to use the wrestling at court as a means of getting rid of Rosader. The bouts have been arranged by the villainous King Torismund to distract his subjects from their attachment to the good king, Gerismond, whose throne he has usurped and who has gone to the Forest of Arden and become an outlaw. The wrestling is described in much more detail than in Shakespeare's text, which of course leaves the action to be staged.

With that Rosader vailed bonnet [doffed his hat] to the King, and lightly leapt within the lists, where noting more the company than the combatant, he cast his eye upon the troupe of ladies that glistered there like the stars of heaven, but at last Love, willing to make him as amorous as he was valiant, presented him with the sight of Rosalynde, whose admirable beauty so inveigled the eye of Rosader, that forgetting himself, he stood and fed his looks on the favour of Rosalynde's face, which she perceiving, blushed; which was such a doubling of her beauteous excellence, that the bashful red of Aurora at her sight of unacquainted Phaeton was not half so glorious. The Norman seeing this young Gentleman fettered in the looks of the Ladies, drove him out of his memento [reverie] with a shake by the shoulder. Rosader looking back with an angry frown, as if he had been awakened from some pleasant dream, discovered to all by the fury of his countenance that he was man of some high thoughts. But when they all noted his youth and the sweetness of his visage, with a general applause of favours; they grieved so goodly a young man should venture in so base an action. But seeing it were to his dishonour to hinder him from his enterprise, they wished him to be graced with the palm of victory. After Rosader was thus called out of his memento [reverie] by the Norman, he roughly clapped to him with so fierce an encounter, that they both fell to the ground, and with the violence of the fall were forced to breathe. In which space the Norman called to mind by all tokens, that this was he whom Saladyne had appointed him to kill. Which conjecture made him stretch every limb and try every sinew, that working his death he might recover the gold, which so bountifully was promised him. On the contrary part, Rosader while he breathed was not idle, but still cast his eye upon Rosalynde, who to encourage him with a favour, lent him such an amorous look, as might have made the most coward desperate. Which glance of Rosalynde so fired the passionate desires of Rosader, that turning to the Norman he ran upon him and braved him with a strong encounter. The Norman received him as valiantly, that there was a sore combat, hard to judge on whose side fortune would be prodigal. At last Rosader called to mind the beauty of his new Mistress, the fame of his Father's honours, and the disgrace that should fall to his house by his misfortune, roused himself and threw the Norman against the ground, falling upon his chest with so willing a weight, that the Norman yielded nature her due, and Rosader the victory.   (pp. 170–1; **compare with I.ii**)

After the bout, Rosader is rewarded by Rosalynde, who has been as taken with him as he with her, though her attidude towards love, it is intimated, has a certain degree of irony and cynicism, a frequent element in romances:

As the King and Lords graced him with embracing, so the Ladies favoured him with their looks, especially Rosalynde, whom the beauty and valour of Rosader had already touched. But she accounted love a toy, and fancy a momentary passion, that as it was taken in with a gaze, might be shaken off with a wink; and therefore feared not to dally in the flame, and to make Rosader know she affected him took from her neck a jewel, and sent it by a Page to the young Gentleman.   (p. 172; **compare with I.ii**)

The two kings are not brothers, as in Shakespeare, and the bad king is not displeased when Rosader kills the Norman. (It is Shakespeare who makes Rosalind's and Orlando's fathers dear friends, thus creating a link between the lovers.) Torismond banishes Rosalynde because he fears that one of his peers will marry her, use her right to the throne as justification and attempt to overthrow him. Alinda (Celia) is also banished by the king, rather than deciding herself to join her friend. The two girls decide to disguise themselves as a lady and her page, 'Aliena' and 'Ganimede', and set off for the Forest of Arden, where they wander for several days, 'being often in danger of wild beasts, and pained with many passionate sorrows' (p. 180).

At last Ganimede casting up his eye spied where on a tree was engraven certain verses: which as soon as he spied, he cried out; Be of good cheer Mistress, I spy the figures of men; for here in these trees are engraven certain verses of shepherds, or some other swains that inhabit here about. (p. 180; **compare with III.ii**)

Lodge gives his reader the poem the girls have discovered, called *Montanus Passion*, one of many included in the work. The two girls comment on it.

No doubt (quoth Aliena) this poesie is the passion of some perplexed shepherd, that being enamoured of some fair and beautiful Shepherdess, suffered some sharp repulse, and therefore complained of the cruelty of his Mistress. You may see (quoth Ganimede) what mad cattle you women be, whose hearts are sometimes made of Adamant that will touch with no impression, and sometimes of wax that is fit for every form. They delight to be courted, and then they glory to seem coy. And when they are most desired then they freeze with disdain. And this fault is so common with the sex, that you see it painted in the shepherd's passions, who found his Mistress as forward as he was enamoured. And I pray you (quoth Aliena) if your robes were off, what metal are you made of that you are so satirical against women? Is it not a foul bird defiles the own nest? (**See IV.i.191–4, noting the effect of the roles being played by boys**). Beware (Ganimede) that Rosader hear you not. If he do, perchance you will make him leap so far from love, that he will anger every vein in your heart. Thus (quoth Ganimede) I keep decorum, I speak now as I am Aliena's page, not as I am Gerismond's daughter. For put me but into a petticoat, and I will stand in defiance to the uttermost that women are courteous, constant, virtuous, and what not.   (p. 181; **compare with II.iv. and III.ii**)

Shortly afterwards, they come upon another poem on a tree, this one signed by Montanus (Shakespeare's Silvius). Again, Lodge uses the opportunity for the girls to comment on the behaviour of the sexes, with Ganimede again critical of the female character:

No doubt (quoth Ganimede) this protestation grew from one full of passions. I am of that mind too (quoth Aliena) but see I pray, when poor women seek to keep themselves chaste, how men woo them with many feigned promises, alluring with sweet words as the Sirens, and after proving as trothless as Aeneas. Thus promised Demoophon to his Phillis, but who at last grew more false? The reason was (quoth Ganimede) that they were women's sons, and took that fault of their mother. For if man had grown from man, as Adam did from the earth, men had never been troubled with inconstancy. Leave off (quoth Aliena) to taunt thus bitterly, or else I'll pull off your page's apparel and whip you (as Venus doth her wantons) with nettles. So you will (quoth Ganimede) persuade me to flattery, that needs not. But come (seeing we have found here by this Fountain the track of shepherds by their Madrigals and Roundelays) let us forward. For either we shall find some folds, sheepcotes, or else some cottages wherein for a day or two to rest. Content (quoth Aliena) and with that they rose up, and marched forward till towards evening. And then coming into a fair valley (compassed with mountains, whereon grew many pleasant shrubs) they might descry where two flocks of sheep did feed. Then looking about they might perceive where an old shepherd sat (and with him a young swain) under a covert most pleasantly situated. (pp. 182–3)

These are the old man, Corydon, with Montanus, the lovesick shepherd, engaged in a poetic dialogue about love (**compare II.iv.20–40**). The latter offers Ganimede and Aliena his master's farm and flock: 'cheap you may have them for ready money' (p. 188) and the opportunity to live the pastoral life. They accept with pleasure.

By my troth shepherd (quoth Aliena) thou makest me in love with your country life, and therefore send for thy Landlord, and I will buy thy farm and thy flocks, & thou shalt still (under me) be overseer of them both: only for pleasure sake I and my Page will serve you, lead the flocks to the field, and fold them. Thus will I live quiet, unknown, and contented. (p. 189; **compare II.iv.41–98**)

Meanwhile, Saladyne tries again to get rid of his brother by seizing him as he sleeps, tying him to a post, refusing him food and declaring him mad. Old Adam Spencer rescues him and, after enlisting the help of the sheriff of the county, Rosader escapes with Adam to the forest, where they soon lose their way. The young hero comes at last upon the exiled King Gerismond feasting with his lords and is accepted into his service for his father's sake (**compare II.vii.194–200**).

Meanwhile, Torismond seizes the revenues of Saladyne and Rosader and puts the elder brother in prison because he has wronged the younger. Saladyne then begins to regret his treatment of his younger brother and wishes to find some means of penance. When he is released by King Torismond and banished, Saladyne, 'grieving at his exile, yet determined to bear it with patience, and in penance of his former follies to travel abroad in every Coast till he had found out his brother Rosader' (p. 199; **compare IV.iii.95–141 and** *passim*).

Rosader, now living with Torismond and his outlaws, wanders the forest and one day, like Montanus, engraves a sonnet on the bark of a tree and generally moons about, crying out the name of Rosalynde **(compare III.ii)**. He is seen by Ganimede and Aliena, who hail him and mock him for his sentimental love. Ganimede especially insists that his Rosalynde cannot be as perfect as he makes her out to be in his verses. She is so cruel to him that, when they are again alone, Aliena chides her for her harshness. But Ganimede responds in her person as page: 'Ah Aliena (quoth she) be not peremptory in your judgements, I hear Rosalynde praised as I am Ganimede, but were I Rosalynde, I could answer the forester: If he mourn for love, there are medicines for love. . . .' (p. 204; **compare III.ii.388–413**).

The next day, Ganimede/Rosalynde rouses Aliena early from her sleep so that they can go and find Rosader so she may continue mocking him about his love. 'Take heed, Forester,' she tells him, 'step not too far, the ford may be deep, and you slip over the shoes; I tell thee, flies have their spleen, the ants choler, the least hares [have] shadows, the smallest loves great desires. 'Tis good (Forester) to love, but not to overlove. . . .' (p. 206; **compare III.ii.350–92**). Ganimede tries to persuade him to give up his hopeless love for Rosalynde and woo Aliena, but he declines and they continue their extended discussions of love, including new sonnets by Rosader. They invite him to have dinner with them, and they have

. . . such cates as Country state did allow them, sauced with such content, and such sweet prattle, as it seemed far more sweet than all their Courtly junkets. As soon as they had taken their repast, Rosader giving them thanks for his good cheer, would have been gone. But Ganimede, that was loth to let him pass out of her presence, began thus: Nay Forester, quoth

he, if thy business be not the greater, seeing Thou sayest thou art so
deeply in love, let me see how thou canst woo (**compare IV.i.65ff**). I will
represent Rosalynde, and thou shalt be as thou art, Rosader. See in some
amorous Eclogue, how if Rosalynde were present, how thou couldst
court her. . . .   (p. 211; **compare III.ii.414–15**)

Whereupon there is a lengthy poetic dialogue between Rosader and
Ganimede as Rosalynde, following which,

> Ganimede . . . began to be thus pleasant: How now Forester, have I not
> fitted your turn? Have I not played the woman handsomely, and showed
> myself as coy in grants, as courteous in desires, and been as full of suspi-
> cion, as men of flattery? And yet to save all, jumped I not all up with the
> sweet union of love? Did not Rosalynde content her Rosader? (**Compare
> IV.i.84–6**). The Forester at this smiling, shook his head, and folding his
> arms made this merry reply. Truth, gentle Swain, Rosader hath his
> Rosalynde: but as Ixion had Juno, who thinking to possess a goddess,
> only embraced a cloud; in these imaginary fruitions of fantasy I resemble
> the birds that fed themselves with Zeuxis' painted grapes. . . . So fareth it
> with me, who to feed myself with the hope of my Mistress' favours. Sooth
> myself in my suits, and only in conceit reap a wished for content. But if
> my food be no better than such amorous dreams, Venus at the year's end
> shall find me but a lean lover. Yet do I take these follies for high fortunes,
> and hope these feigned affections do divine some unfeigned end of ensu-
> ing fancies (**compare IV.i.85–6**). And thereupon (quoth Aliena) I'll play
> the priest: from this day forth Ganimede shall call thee husband, and thou
> shalt call Ganimede wife, and so we'll have a marriage. Content (quoth
> Rosader) and laughed. Content (quoth Ganimede) and changed as red as
> a rose. And so with a smile and a blush, they made up this jesting match,
> that after proved to a marriage in earnest; Rosader full little thinking he
> had wooed and won his Rosalynde. But all was well, hope is a sweet string
> to harp on.   (pp. 213–14; **compare IV.i.117ff**)

Rosader goes away from his pleasant play with Ganimede and
Aliena, and passing through the forest comes upon his brother
Saladyne, exhausted by his wanderings, asleep under a tree and being
watched by a crouching lion. He debates at length with himself
whether to save his cruel brother. Finally deciding to do so, he kills
the lion. Saladyne wakes, but does not recognize his rescuer. He tells

the apparent stranger about his contrition for having so mistreated his brother. At last he recognizes him and there is a lengthy reconciliation: 'Much ado there was between these two Brethren, Saladyne in craving pardon, and Rosader in forgiving and forgetting all former injuries.' (pp. 215–19). Rosader takes his brother to meet Gerismond, who welcomes him to his service (**compare IV.iii.98–144**).

Shortly afterwards, Rosader, accompanied by Saladyne, goes to visit the girls in the forest. They are just in time to rescue Alinda from a band of outlaws who were trying to abduct her as a present for Torismond, unaware that she is his daughter. Alinda and Saladyne fall in love, though Alinda worries whether he will continue to love her when he learns she is the daughter of the evil Torismond. She has lengthy discussions with Rosalynde and they finally agree that all will be well. There follow extended discussions about love between Saladyne and Alinda, culminating in his proposal of marriage.

At this point, Corydon comes running to them, saying that, knowing they have long wanted to see Montanus's beloved Phoebe, he will now take them to see Montanus courting her with 'his country ditties' (p. 227; **compare III.iv.43ff**). They hurry to the scene and, hiding behind some bushes, watch an extended scene (pp. 227–31; **compare III.v.1ff**) in which the shepherd sings his poems to Phoebe and she replies with a sonnet of rejection. Hearing all this, Ganimede bursts from his hiding place to berate Phoebe for her cruelty. She is taken with his beauty and when he at last leaves, she gives him 'such an adieu with a piercing glance, that the amorous Girle-boy perceived Phoebe was pinched by the heel' (p. 233). Phoebe is so smitten that she becomes genuinely ill, and finally writes him a letter, with a sonnet enclosed (pp. 239–41; **compare III.v.81ff**). Feeling sorry for her, Ganimede goes to her and tells her he cannot love her. But he also tries to console her – 'thou mayest see I disdain not though I desire not' (p. 245; **compare IV.iii**) – and urges her to accept Montanus. Finally, repenting her forwardness, she tells Ganimede that 'when reason . . . doth quench that love that I owe to thee, then will I fancy Montanus' (p. 245; **compare V.iv.11–15**). And Ganimede replies, 'I will never marry myself to woman but unto thyself' (p. 245; **compare V.ii.112–15**).

When Rosader learns of his brother's marriage, he is sad

(**compare V.ii.42–45**) and Ganimede tells him, 'I have a friend that is deeply experienced in Necromancy and Magic, what art can do shall be acted for thine advantage: I will cause him to bring in Rosalynde, if either France or any bordering nation harbour her' (p. 246; **compare V.ii.51–68**).

The wedding day arrives (**compare V.iv**, *passim*). Rosalynde as Ganimede arranges everything, but without revealing her true identity to either her father or Rosader. Montanus appears, dressed in sad attire, and sings of his woe at being rejected. Ganimede departs briefly and returns as Rosalynde. There is a tearful reunion with her father, who gives her in marriage to Rosader. Rosalynde then turns to Phoebe and asks her if what has happened has been a sufficient reason for her to change her love. 'Yea, quoth Phoebe, so great a persuasive, that, please it you Madame and Aliena to give us leave, Montanus and I will make this day the third couple in marriage' (p. 253; **compare V.iv.148–9**). The couples are married. Coridon provides a feast and, bringing on an old fiddler, sings them a happy country song.

Coridon having thus made them merry, as they were in the midst of all their jollity, word was brought in to Saladyne and Rosader that a brother of theirs, one Fernandyne, was arrived and desired to speak with them. Gerismond, overhearing this news, demanded who it was? It is sir (quoth Rosader), our middle brother, that lives a scholar in Paris. But what fortune hath driven him to seek us out I know not. With that, Saladyne went and met his brother, whom he welcomed with all courtesy, and Rosader gave him no less friendly entertainment. Brought he was by his two brothers into the parlour where they all sat at dinner. Fernandyne, as one that knew as many manners as he could [know] points of sophistry, and was as well brought up as well lettered, saluted them all. But when he espied Gerismond, kneeling on his knee he did him what reverence belonged to his estate, and with that burst forth into these speeches. Although (right mighty Prince) this day my brothers' marriage be a day of mirth, yet time craves another course, and therefore from dainty cates rise to sharp weapons. And you the sons of Sir John of Bordeaux, leave off your amours and fall to arms, change your loves into lances, and now this day show yourselves as valiant as hitherto you have been passionate. For know Gerismond, that hard by at the edge of this forest twelve Peers of France are up in arms to recover thy right, and Torismond trouped with a crew of desperate renegades is ready to bid them battle. The Armies are ready to join, therefore show thyself in the field to encourage thy subjects. And you Saladyne & Rosader mount you, and show yourselves as hardy soldiers as you have been hearty lovers. So shall you for the benefit of your Country, discover the Idea of your father's virtues to be stamped in your thoughts, and prove children worthy of so honourable a parent. At this alarm given by Fernandyne, Gerismond leapt from the board, and Saladyne and Rosader betook themselves to their weapons. Nay, quoth Gerismond, go with me, I have horse and armour for us all, and then being well mounted, let us show that we carry revenge and honour at our falchions' [broadswords'] points. Thus they leave the brides full of sorrow, especially Alinda, who desired Gerismond to be good to her father: he not returning a word because his haste was great, hied him home to his lodge, where he delivered Saladyne and Rosader horse and armour, and himself armed royally led the way: not having ridden two leagues before they discovered where in a Valley both the battles were joined. Gerismond seeing the wing wherein the Peers fought, thrust in there, and cried St Denis, Gerismond laying on such load upon his enemies, that he showed how highly he did estimate of a Crown. When the Peers perceived that their rightful King was there, they grew more eager. And Saladyne and Rosader so behaved themselves, that none durst stand in their way, nor abide the fury of their weapons. To be short, the Peers were conquerors, Torismond's army put to flight, & himself slain in battle. The Peers then gathered themselves together, and saluting their king, conducted him royally to Paris, where he was received with great joy of all the citizens. As soon as all was quiet and he had received again the Crown, he sent for Alinda and Rosalynde to the court, Alinda being very passionate for the death of her father, yet brooking it with more patience, in that she was contented with the welfare of her Saladyne. Well, as soon as they were come to Paris, Gerismond made a royal feast for the Peers and Lords of his land, which continued thirty days, in which time summoning a Parliament, by the consent of his Nobles he created Rosader heir apparent to the kingdom. He restored Saladyne to all his father's land, and gave him the Dukedom of Nemours. He made Fernandyne principal secretary to himself, and that Fortune might every way seem frolic, he made Montanus Lord over all the Forest of Arden, Adam Spencer Captain of the King's Guard, and Coridon Master of Alinda's flocks.   (pp. 255–6)

The structural changes made by Shakespeare to this tale are interesting. Lodge's narrative is detailed and sequential, with frequent references to the time of day and the passage of time, while Shakespeare famously ignores the passage of time (see Jay Halio's essay, below, pp. 152–3). By placing everything in a timeless present, he removes the sense that this is a narrative dependent on natural causality. (The handling of time in a stage play will always be very different, of course, from that in a purely literary narrative.) Lodge, working in the genre of the romance, has his characters breaking into verse or song frequently and at length, while Shakespeare has almost eliminated the use of love poetry, treating it satirically when he does. Most importantly, he has greatly altered the comparative importance of the characters. Lodge's Alinda is nearly as important as Rosalynde, while Shakespeare has changed the balance entirely, except for the early scenes of the play. Comparably, he has reduced the love of Saladyne (Oliver) and Alinda (Celia) to the briefest of subplots, hardly troubling to explain how it came about. Phoebe and Montanus (Silvius) have not only shrunk in importance, but are treated far more satirically. The two kings, unrelated, Shakespeare makes into dukes and brothers, underlining the parallel with the Orlando–Oliver story.

With all these changes, however, it is still striking how much Shakespeare's characterizations owe to Lodge's originals. Particularly interesting is his adoption and use of the ironic attitude towards love displayed by Rosalynde. His central character becomes an adaptation of the typical romance heroine, but with this central attitude developed into a rich and mature realism balancing the sentimental passion of traditional romantic love. It is also important to note Shakespeare's ironic use of the boy player in the Rosalind role as a means of further, metatheatrical commentaries on role-playing, the follies of love and issues of gender.

The most remarked-upon changes made by Shakespeare are his insertion of several new characters, most importantly Touchstone and Jaques, but also including Audrey, William, and Sir Oliver Martext. (His addition of Amiens may have been primarily to provide a role for Armin to display his singing skills.) These five are all very theatrical figures, one or another kind of clown or fool, of varying degrees of sophistication. They also add an important perspective to our view of the main characters by serving as foils, as well as providing additional examples of wit and folly. Finally, it is worth noting that the addition of these characters, along with their lines of action, provides dramatic material to interpolate within and between the scenes of the main plot, making it easier to handle that plot more selectively and episodically.

The examination of the contexts in which the play was created helps us not only to connect it to its time and to the work of other writers, but to see even more clearly the particular skills Shakespeare brings to bear. What might have been another pastoral romance or popular 'hodge-podge' becomes a far more integrated and theatrical work, skilfully making use of the distinctive resources of actors and public theatre, while at the same time taking themes and characters from a traditional form and giving them a new, livelier and more complex kind of life. Most of all, he has taken the material of a successful literary source and, adding elements from his own theatrical imagination, transformed it into a complex performance work with a unique flavour.

3 Commentary: the Play in Performance

Introduction

The play's sequential structure

As You Like It resembles a kind of dramatic collage not only in the different kinds of dramatic action it represents, but also in its episodic, almost cinematic structure. Most scenes are short – some little more than vignettes (II.vi) or entertainment interludes (IV.ii) – with longer, more developed and sustained sequences occurring only rarely. The tempo of the scenes is nearly always quick, largely because there are very few long speeches. The dialogue consists almost entirely of comparatively quick exchanges: out of a total of 806 individual character speeches in the play, only 50 are of 10 lines or more, that is, approximately 30 seconds. As a result of this brevity, scenes generally move with a very musical fluidity.

To perceive the play's performance sequence, we must look beyond the traditional Act and scene divisions. A clearer idea of the play as a continuous action can be gained from considering the structural elements we are most conscious of in performance: what may be called **action units**. An action unit begins and ends with any significant change of subject or direction in the stage action, often with the introduction of a new character into the scene. For example, Act I, scene i (171 lines, with an estimated playing time of about 8½ minutes) is divided into five action units: lines 1–25 (Orlando and Adam), 26–84 (Orlando and Oliver, Adam mostly listening), 85–94 (Oliver alone and with Dennis), 95–161 (Oliver and Charles), and 161–71 (Oliver alone). In other words, a textual scene lasting about 8½ minutes actually breaks down into action units of approximately 1 minute, 3 minutes, half a minute, 3 minutes and half a minute. In the entire play of twenty-two scenes, plus Epilogue, there is a total of fifty-four action units, varying in length from 5 lines (15 seconds) to 154 lines (7½ minutes). The average length is under 60 lines, or less than 3 minutes.

The effects of these frequent changes of action on the pace and effect of the whole performance are considerable. They also influence the handling and development of character interplay. With the single exception of Rosalind and Orlando, character relationships are presented through brief scenes of interaction.

The play's dramatic structure: plots

The central and most conspicuous element in the play's dramatic structure – the play's dramatic spine – is of course the main love plot involving Rosalind and Orlando. For part of the play, this is a double-stranded construction. Initially, each character has an action line or plot, but they join briefly, early in the play (I.ii), are separated (after I.ii), then join again (from III.ii.290) and remain so until the end of the play. This main plot does not occupy the action of every scene, however, although its central figures, Rosalind and Orlando, figure separately in most of the subplots, of which there are five.

The first of these is very slight, laying out the action of Oliver in his relations with Orlando, Duke Frederick and, towards the end, with Rosalind's dear friend Celia. Another subplot involves the interplay of Silvius, Phebe and Rosalind as 'Ganymede', a satirical version of a typical pastoral romance. A third subplot centres on Touchstone, the clown. For much of the play, he functions only as a comic commentator, but at the end of Act III he becomes engaged in the comical courtship of Audrey. The last of the play's subplots is of a different kind. While it lacks a distinct dramatic objective, it none the less has a coherence of its own. This is the action of Jaques, who makes several appearances as the upper-class 'court jester' in the forest court of Duke Senior, adopts the clown Touchstone as his protégé and engages in a series of prickly meetings with other major characters. His subplot is 'resolved' when he abandons the court to take up a sequestered life. The Jaques subplot is one aspect of the pastoral life of Duke Senior, which constitutes a shadow subplot accompanying the other actions in the Forest and ending with the restoration of his dukedom.

There is some interaction between these seven lines of action, several characters having roles in one or more plots. The main plot and subplots are interwoven in the course of the play and brought together only in the final scenes. Even the Rosalind–Orlando plot does not figure in every scene, though it does of course dominate the play as a whole. Shakespeare's basic method is to keep the main plot sufficiently in the foreground so that we do not lose touch with it, but to interrupt it with elements from lesser plot actions to provide variety and suspense. With the exception of two long Rosalind–Orlando scenes (III.ii. and IV.i), no single plot holds the stage for more than a few minutes at a time.

The play's dramatic structure: locales

The basic progression of locales in *As You Like It* reveals a very broad outline of the action, at first narrow and constricted, then becoming more free and open. The early locales are expressions of the characters controlling them, Oliver and Duke Frederick, who get the main plot under way by forcing the hero and heroine to escape and seek freedom. Having served this purpose, these locales effectively disappear about a quarter of the way through the play (after II.iii, except for a very brief flashback in III.i).

With the move to the Forest of Arden, the structure of the dramatic action changes considerably, loosening and altering its tone. Now the play's dominant (and after III.i its only) locale, Arden is the place where the hero and heroine can pursue their desires and encounter new characters and circumstances. Within this general locale, the action flows freely and episodically from place to place. Particular locations within the forest are either unspecific sites where characters happen to meet or locations identified by an association with particular characters, such as the 'campsite court' of Duke Senior or, later, the area near Rosalind and Celia's cottage. Most of these tend to be associated with characters who make them their 'homes': Duke Senior, Rosalind, Silvius and Phebe, Touchstone and

Audrey. The fluidity of the movement from place to place within Arden expresses the shifting of focus from character to character. The variety of different kinds of characters and events occurring in this broad locale gives it a flexible indeterminacy exactly equivalent to that of the stage itself. The sublocales within the forest have no distinctive physical characteristics of foliage or ground, but are given their distinctive qualities only by the characters who occupy them, who are all essentially comic. The Forest of Arden is itself therefore a comic locale, except in two scenes. The only times the Forest shows its teeth, as it were, are when serious characters (Adam and Orlando in II.vi, Oliver and Orlando in IV.iii) presume it to have a hostile life of its own, rather than treating it (as characters otherwise do) as a natural arena for comic action. Given its variety and fluidity, we conclude that the Forest of Arden is not primarily a place, but a presiding state of mind, within which there is a succession of particular feelings of place.

When it is important for the audience to know where the fictional action is taking place, it is revealed by characters mentioning it in the dialogue, usually only to make clear a change from the preceding scene. As the play progresses and the characters' actions need less and less to be explicitly located, such references begin to disappear. After the end of Act II, fictional locale is barely mentioned in the dialogue at all. Locational references are replaced by a tone of speech and/or behaviour which implies the kind of place where the action is happening.

The play's dramatic structure: character plots

From one important perspective, the dramatic structure of any play is a composite of the actions of its characters, not only as interactions comprising story plots, but as the individual action sequences of each character, which are the building blocks of dramatic structure. Character plots are in themselves distinct constructs. To trace their development is not only helpful in understanding the over-all structure of the play, but forms an essential part of the work of actors and directors. For actors particularly it is often important to formulate the character's objectives, or through line.

While such essentially Stanislavskian analysis of character plot is useful, it can result in an over-schematization of character, which can sometimes be fatal to its life. Such an approach can also lead the actor to forget that character is often a function of plot: the characters do what they do simply because the plot requires it (see, for example, Rosalind's relationship with her father). The development of a dramatic character is not always so logical as analysis can make it seem. The fullest realization of a character only comes into existence in performance, arising out of the interaction between actors and between actors and audience. Like getting to know a person in life, the creation of a character in a play is a cumulative, moment-to-moment thing, gradually adding up (sometimes quite mysteriously) to a particular experience the actor and audience *feel* is what this character 'is'. Present-day actors of Shakespeare have commented on this way of perceiving character. Harriet Walter, for example, has offered a clear and practical account: 'You play each scene or each beat, however contradictory, or however incompatible it seems with what has gone before or what comes after. Then, by the end of the play, the character is an accumulation of all those separate moments' (Rutter, 1988, p. 76).

In some plays, the action of the main character is regarded as virtually the same as the complete dramatic plot of the play. This happens more often with tragedies (for example, *Hamlet* or *Othello*) than with comedies. Rosalind's action is sometimes treated as if it were the entire plot of *As You Like It*, but this can lead to a misapprehension of the real structure of the play. Every character plot – not least Rosalind's – is intertwined with other character plots, even sometimes with those that seem little connected dramatically. This is especially apparent with Rosalind, a 'double character' whose action is interwoven with those of at least six other characters. This interconnectedness reminds us again that the play is not simply a vehicle for one character.

To perceive the interrelationship of character plots with each other and with the overall structure, it is helpful to look at the pattern of onstage appearances by the various characters, as an indication of the relation between the rhythm of their individual actions and that of the play in performance as a whole.

The play's theatrical structure

The essential theatrical structure of *As You Like It* can be seen in the scene-to-scene progression of the play. Scenes are always started by the entrance onto the stage of one or more characters and finished with the departure of those remaining at the end: as the scene opens, people are coming from somewhere; as it closes, they are going somewhere. In performance, this practice creates an impression of a structured continuity between offstage and onstage action. Characters (and thus actors) are always moving on and off the stage – and of course around the stage – giving us a sense of a perpetual flow of people as the performance progresses. These currents are comparatively rapid. With the exception of one scene, no set of characters is on the stage for longer than twelve minutes at a time (the average is much less). This ebb and flow of people on the stage gives the whole play in performance an essentially transient dynamic.

Another dominant feature of the play's theatrical structure is the multiplicity of performance styles it involves. Actors are required to play serious drama, lyrical romance, witty repartee, satire and farce. In addition, the play requires performers to be able to sing, dance and (in the case of two of them) wrestle. While not every actor will be required to perform in all these ways, most will be capable of a number of different performing skills (as were most actors in an Elizabethan company).

The play also requires its actors not only to portray more or less believable characters, but also to perform in an openly theatrical manner. Such presentational elements, to be noted in the following commentary, are frequent. Fifteen of the play's twenty-two scenes include performers' set-pieces of one kind or another, most of which contribute little or nothing to advancing the dramatic plot. These include obviously presentational elements like songs, a dance and a wrestling match, as well as a considerable number of other sequences where comic characters perform stage routines whose primary purpose is pure entertainment. Such sequences occur with increasing frequency after Act II, scene iii, when the two branches of the main plot are well under way. From that point onwards, Shakespeare creates a pattern of presentational sequences paralleling the main dramatic actions, perhaps to slow down the play's dramatic momentum and reduce our serious emotional identification with the characters' fictional lives. Of the approximately 138 minutes of the play's complete performance, more than half (about 76 minutes) are occupied with unmistakably performative and/or metatheatrical action. Clearly, *As You Like It* is not only a fictional construct; it is also a carefully structured performance piece.

The play as metatheatre

Another essential component of the play as a performance is its metatheatricality, that is, those elements in the play which intentionally remind the audience that it is watching a performance. Metatheatre, sometimes called 'theatre about theatre', is far more common in *As You Like It* than in other Shakespearean comedies. It takes three common forms in the play.

The first occurs when the representation of the fictional action is interrupted by purely presentational entertainment with little or no dramatic content – for example, a song or a dance. When such a performance is presented by actors in character, their primary onstage function becomes a presentational one, and we are aware of them more as performers than as characters.

The second occurs when characters in a scene perform for other characters, who become spectators, and the audience is led to perceive the action as a piece of onstage theatre. When one or more characters perform in this manner, they tend to be seen as both fictional characters and theatrical role-players. There is a small element of this kind of metatheatre whenever a character's speech or a stage direction indicates one or more characters performing, while others – sometimes visible, more often not – watch or listen, thus creating a performer–spectator division on the stage. (Usually, this is initiated by 'stand aside' or its equivalent, a frequent practice in *As You Like It*.)

A third kind of metatheatre, especially common in the play, occurs when an actor, whether playing to onstage spectators or not, is simultaneously perceived by the theatre audience as a dramatic character and, in her/his real-life identity, as an actor on the stage before us. This contradictory duality of dramatic fiction and theatrical actuality is the basic irony of dramatic performance, which is heightened when the player calls attention to her/his doubleness. Sometimes this is done explicitly, the actor deliberately departing from the character to address the audience as a performer, as partially happens in the Epilogue. More commonly, the actor conveys to the audience her/his awareness of their presence and her/his own actorliness, even while 'staying in character', so that what occurs is that the *character* becomes a theatrical identity addressing the spectators (who readily accept the dual identity of the person talking to them). Audience address of this kind is very rarely used in serious drama, which usually requires a sustained belief in the fictional person. In comedy, on the other hand, audience belief is often fluid and the genre is therefore inherently metatheatrical. In *As You Like It*, there is no significant metatheatre until the action reaches the Forest of Arden and becomes both comic and metatheatrical. Audience address works best when the character is a 'performer' in the fictional world, as are Touchstone, Rosalind and Jaques in particular. Since all three of these characters frequently give performances for other characters, the performers of the roles can more easily address the theatrical audience as well. (The commentary will point out instances of this through the play.)

Frequent and frank acknowledgement of the audience's presence was normal in the original staging of Elizabethan comedy. It was a particularly important element in the performances of clowns, as well as of the boy player of the Rosalind role (for extended discussion of this, see Soule, 2000, pp. 115–75). Despite the strong tradition of realistic acting in modern theatre, theatrical performance in recent years has become much less rigorously illusionistic, so that today's spectators – especially younger ones – tend to welcome such metatheatrical flexibility on the part of the actor as a lively enrichment of the theatrical event.

Scene-by-scene commentary

The Elizabethan playwright John Marston wrote that it 'afflicted' him that 'scenes invented merely to be spoken should be enforcively published to be read' (Marston, 1887, vol. 1, p. 198). 'Comedy,' he added, 'whose life rests much in the actor's voice, [is] writ to be spoken' (ibid., vol. 2, p. 110). *As You Like It* in performance consists mainly of people simply talking to each other (and to the audience). It is therefore important to remember how very physical stage talk can be. Voices and speech – including elements such as timbre, energy and tempo, dexterity and feeling – and their employment of the actor's whole body comprise the basic dynamics of the stage action. The Rosalind role illustrates this most brilliantly, but it is evident in every other part as well. In *As You Like It*, therefore, even when the actors' bodies move comparatively little around the stage, they are always engaged in some kind of lively physical and psychological action. It is this action of which the text is a suggestion and a partial record.

The commentary is based on the Arden edition of the play, edited by Agnes Latham. The scene timings are estimates. Line numbers at the left margin indicate sections to which commentaries relate.

ACT I

Act I, scene i (171 lines; approx. 8 minutes)

The scene is intense, fast-moving and – briefly – violent. In a modern production, it would probably be lit harshly, to heighten the strength and darkness of the brothers' anger and Oliver's plotting. Such directness and emotional intensity are not what are expected in a romantic comedy; the scene feels instead like the opening of a serious realistic drama, possibly even a tragedy.

The language is prose, and, in the early part of the scene, frequent animal references remind us that we are on a farm. In general, the language is rhythmically irregular, suggesting the strong feelings of the brothers, a pattern temporarily broken by Charles's more orderly account of the court news and of the reason for his visit, but resuming as Oliver warns the wrestler of Orlando's villainy, and when left alone he speaks strongly of his feelings towards his brother and his intention to get him killed.

The acting in the opening scene of any play is particularly important, because it establishes the style and tone we will tend to expect as
the play progresses. The actors in this scene have to be aware that,
though their characters' action is serious and intense, what is to
follow is a comedy of much variety, and eventually they will both
change greatly. While playing their roles convincingly, therefore,
they will want to keep their characters from being too deeply
unpleasant. One way to do this is to make the hostility between them
very unthinking, a feeling of the moment. Another is to play the
scene at a fairly quick pace, stressing immediate impulsive responses,
though of course this is more difficult with the calculating Oliver.
The gentle faithfulness of Adam is an important contrasting element
in the scene, but the actor will want to avoid playing the role too
sentimentally. Charles can be played with a certain professional cool-
ness, even cynicism, though not so lightly that the threat he poses to
Orlando is diminished.

1–26 The action is strong and quickly becomes violent. Orlando
bursts onto the stage and angrily ranges about. The old servant
listens with concern, at the same time looking fearfully around lest
Oliver should come. Two important sets of social contrasts underlie
Orlando's language here and throughout the scene. One is between
the state of a peasant and that of a gentleman; the other between
fathers and sons and between brothers.

29–84 Oliver is immediately provocative: his 'sir' is how a squire
would address a peasant. Orlando is extremely touchy on the subject
of being born a gentleman (see a similar sensitivity expressed in
II.vii.95–119).

29 The locale of the scene is made clear, while at the same time
Oliver confirms that Orlando's inferior status gives him no rights.

52–77 The stage direction is not in the original text. It is not
absolutely clear who strikes the first blow, Oliver in response to
Orlando's slur in lines 49–51 or Orlando reacting to Oliver's in line 52,
though probably it is the latter. While it is Oliver's insults that have

provoked his violence, it is interesting that Orlando uses his respect for their father as his justification. However it may start, the fight between them wants to be effectively staged. As lines 53–4 suggest, Orlando is well aware that he is far more skilful and experienced at fighting than his brother. He immediately puts a powerful grip on Oliver, holding him firm (perhaps by the throat and arm), however much he struggles to get free. We see here that Orlando is a very skilled and strong wrestler whose challenge of a professional like Charles has not just been the wishful thinking of an isolated youth. His victory in the next scene (though it is a fairy-tale outcome) should seem credible.

95–161   Oliver's hypocrisy is made apparent. His manner with Charles is entirely different from how he has spoken earlier. At first politely ingratiating to a social inferior whose help he wants, his manner then hardens. As he is increasingly caught up in winning the wrestler's cooperation, his emotional description of Orlando becomes more and more extreme.

98–119   Charles's exposition introduces the other major narrative of the play, while also, in its reference to Duke Senior's happy exile in the Forest of Arden and the brief descriptions of Rosalind and Celia, preparing for later action more suitable to comedy. The rivalry of two Dukes for power, wealth and land is also clearly implied, a conflict parallel to the one in this scene.

105–12   A similarity between Orlando and Rosalind is implicitly established: both have been recently deprived of a father and both are unhappy when we first meet them, which (romantic comedy being what it is) is a conventional prelude to their eventual happiness.

114–19   Here, and in line 141, the play's other locales are introduced. The action occurs in France, near the court of a duke, a place likely to be defined by arbitrary authority. The other important locale, the Forest of Arden, likened to 'the golden world' (l. 119), is where the banished duke and his followers 'live like the old Robin Hood of England' (ll. 115–16). This touch of the legendary creates an expectation of a place quite different from the immediate, arbitrary world of Oliver and Duke Frederick.

161–71 Ironically, it is from Oliver that we learn of Orlando's nobler, gentler side, which we have not yet seen. Oliver's own self-esteem is undermined by his brother's virtue, as he acknowledges to himself. Is there in this self-awareness a small hint of the possibility of later repentance and reformation? In Lodge's *Rosalynde*, Saladyne, Oliver's equivalent character, goes through much soul-accusation on the road to reform (see, for example, Bullough, 1963, vol. 2, p. 198).

Act I, scene ii (279 lines; approx. 14 minutes plus wrestling)

This scene provides an abrupt change from the preceding one. At first, the pace and rhythm are lightened and altered: for the first time, the play feels like a comedy. But as the scene progresses and suspense heightens, the mood intensifies in two ways, one essentially comic, the other darker and more serious.

The locale is the ducal court, a place where the audience would expect important events and perhaps sophistication and wit. In such a setting, characters are likely to be on their best public behaviour, displaying a greater awareness of the constraints exerted by ducal authority and the rules of courtly conduct. The nature of the space may also suggest much general movement: a gathering of people engaged in polite conversation and eager discussions of the coming wrestling match. The acting required is much more varied than in the preceding scene: a mixture of witty high comedy (with an opening touch of light pathos) with later physical action and intense roman-tic feeling.

The audience meets most of the remaining major characters of the play and will form first impressions. With Rosalind, it is her resilience and wit and, most of all, her natural disposition to love which are most conspicuous. Celia's character is very different. She is more wry and sensible, at least in this early scene, as well as being the socially dominant one of the pair (perhaps partly an effect of Shakespeare's source). The difference between the two characters may be because Shakespeare wants to establish Rosalind's greater

susceptibility to feelings (especially love). In these two roles, the celebrated energy and suppleness of the boy players were certainly fully
exploited in the original performances. The modern actor will want
to catch some of the same lively resilience.

It is in this scene that the exceptional fluency and range of the
play's language begins to be demonstrated. The first three-quarters of
the scene is in prose, even though the witty content might seem to
call for a kind of light verse. The language is vigorous and varied,
ranging from the playful banter of Rosalind, Celia and Touchstone to
Orlando's chivalrous speech refusing the young women's plea that
he decline to fight. In the course of the scene, the audience is introduced to the language of courtly conversation and satire, of clowning
and of romance.

3–21   There are three sets of fathers and children in the scene (four
if we include the emblematic old man and his wounded sons).
Rosalind's expression of sadness over her father's unjust banishment roughly parallels Orlando's first speech about his own
mistreatment. Celia ignores her complaint, instead accusing her
friend of not loving her as much as she loves her friend. Her
momentary ill humour is followed by an impulsive switch to loving
generosity. There is a subtextual suggestion here that perhaps Celia
has mixed feelings about her father, which we soon find to be the
case (see ll. 220, 230–1).

24   Introduced for the first time is the key thematic word of the
play: 'love'. This first use is playful and ironic and subtly predicts an
undercurrent in Rosalind's attitude even when most infatuated.

45–84   Touchstone is clearly identified as the professional clown.
To an Elizabethan audience, he would have been well known as one
and would have played to them unashamedly. The same is possible
today, for Touchstone, even as a fictional character, is always playing
to an audience. He is a professional fool, who feels obliged to maintain his reputation by delivering a witty (and usually well-practised)
response to any question (ll. 58–74). He is a public character, who
needs an audience to live. Upon entering, he immediately performs

for Rosalind and Celia, but they may not be enough: he needs the theatre audience as well. Like everything else he does, his entrance itself is probably a practised piece of comic business. Celia's 'Whither wander you?' (l. 54) suggests that he might be making a very circuitous approach to them. His jokey first lines to Celia, spoken almost absent-mindedly, serve mainly to set up the following prepared routine with its emphasized repetition of 'by his honour'. This is followed by another routine – probably accompanied by more physical business and drawing in Rosalind and Celia as stooges (ll. 67–71). The joke about beards and Celia's response to it are clear references to the boy actors playing the roles, though in a modern performance it could be played to the audience as a joke about girls having no beards. All of Touchstone's lines can easily be accompanied by bits of characteristic business and/or movement from the actor's own clown repertoire, in some cases elaborated into one of Touchstone's 'dances' (see below, III.ii.11–84; III.iii.1–98; V.i.1–59; and V.iv.39–102). All of his movement may resemble a kind of dancing. The physical timing will deliberately be just a split second off normal and the basic walk, as is the case with clowns of many kinds, will in itself be a piece of comic movement: it need not be exaggerated or grotesque (like Chaplin's Tramp walk), but something about it will be naturally funny.

Nearly all of Touchstone's lines seem to have been written to be played to the audience at the same time as they are spoken to other characters. This can be done by the modern actor as well. Spectators nowadays are generally not troubled by direct audience address, at least not in a comedy: this is clear in their ready acceptance of the detached, on-and-off impersonations of most present-day stand-up comedians, some of whom might suggest ideas for how to play Touchstone.

109–10 A reminder of the 'tale' of Sir Rowland de Boys and his three sons, serving as a subtle reminder of Orlando's possible fate.

143 She is immediately taken with him. One of the specific tasks facing the actors playing Rosalind and Orlando is to discover during rehearsal at just what point each is struck by 'love at first sight'.

154–9   There is some confusion about which of the young ladies is 'the Princess'. The uncertainty persists until lines 258–73, when Orlando has to ask which is Duke Frederick's daughter. This trivial difficulty with identity continues till the very end of the scene.

156–279   From this point onwards, Orlando's character is developed beyond the opening scene. His claim to be a gentleman is here borne out, as he expresses himself in the language of gallant chivalry to the young women and in his reassertion of his pride in his parentage. There is a brief reminder of his hot-tempered arrogance when he matches taunts with Charles (ll. 190–1, 196–7) and mockingly brags that he is hardly out of breath (ll. 205–6). The primary aspect of his character revealed here, of course, is his capacity for strong and impulsive love combined with a deep shyness.

200   As long as it appears sufficiently threatening and dangerous to justify the fears aroused earlier, the fight can go on as long as director and actors want it to, always assuming it engages the audience and doesn't keep them away from the dramatic action for too long. Some recent productions have made it a big event, with extreme celebrations of Orlando's victory carrying on for some time after the fight. The wrestling match is an obvious metatheatrical element in the scene, a fact emphasized by creating – if only by a ring of spectators – what is in effect a stage within the stage. The entire scene revolves around this primary piece of metatheatre, which is also the dramatic centre, for it shows Orlando performing a kind of romantic audition for Rosalind's love. Both Charles and Orlando will be perceived not only as characters but also as athletes. Orlando becomes a combatant–performer faced with a ritual test of manhood. Rosalind is the audience's surrogate on stage; it is her response to his performance with which we most identify – we are hardly neutral spectators.

212   This is a crucial moment in the play, which will need some kind of emphasis in performance, perhaps by a significant pause before line 213 as the Duke registers Orlando's information. His hostility to Orlando begins here. He might remain seated, his silence and stillness immediately threatening, or alternatively, rise and move away before turning back to Orlando. His change of attitude is expressed in his sudden shift to verse. From this point, the tone of the scene is quite different; the mood darkens and our sense of the Duke's character begins to change. Even though he maintains a cool politeness for the present, the actor of the role will have suggested earlier the hidden depths which now begin to be seen. The audience's response to the character will suddenly shift in this crucial few moments.

214–15 A possible explanation of this is offered in II.vii.198–9. We also note a parallel with Oliver's declared reason for hating Orlando (I.i.164–9). Shakespeare's villains often acknowledge the pure irrationality of their hatred: Richard III, Iago and Edmond, for example, all confirm their wickedness by hating goodness.

220, 230–1 Further evidence of Celia's conflicting feelings about her father (note the relation to lines 7–13, and the exchange between them in I.iii.62–83).

235–48 Here the subject of romantic love is linked to contrasts in characterization. While one lover (the supposedly stronger one) is struck dumb and paralysed by falling in love, the other (the supposedly weaker sex) is enlivened and emboldened by it. These contrasting responses are used to initiate an extended action in which the sentimental pathos of conventional pastoral love and the witty love play of satirical comedy are placed in ironic counterpoint. This brief exchange also introduces another important theme in the play: the role of women. Aside from farce, where female approaches of a bold and bawdy kind were a strong tradition, the woman's taking the initiative in love, when it occurred at all, was commonly achieved under cover of a masculine disguise. This added a touch of daring to the amatory enterprise, while also satirizing the convention of male enterprise in love. Here, however, it is worth noting that even in this early scene, feminine initiative doesn't require disguise – though, significantly, Rosalind is empowered by her superior status.

256 Duke Frederick is somewhat more interesting than a straightforward villain. Le Beau implies that his true nature is too awful to be spoken of, but there are contradictions. It has been said that he is fond of Rosalind (I.i.110–11) and he addresses her equally with Celia when he first enters, though later his feelings about her are shown to be quite different (ll. 263–73). His assertion that he has tried to dissuade Orlando from the bout (I.ii.149) may be sincere, and his insistence that the bout be of only one fall may arise from genuine concern for Orlando. Even after learning Orlando's parentage, he has given him his due as 'a gallant youth' (l. 218). All of the foregoing might be regarded as the hypocrisy of a villain, though one must ask: Why would he be against Orlando before knowing who he is? The more interesting option for the actor may be to consider such contradictions as parts of a complex and unstable character. Until the moment he learns of Orlando's parentage, the only clear evidence of the darkness of his character is the fact that he has usurped his brother's title and estates. The actor of the role will want to think not only about how to play these contradictions, but perhaps also how to reconcile all this with Duke Frederick's remarkable transformation as described in the final scene of the play. The actor might want to remember other actors' comments on the freedom to be inconsistent in dramatic characterization (see above, p. 42).

279   The audience might wonder for a moment how Orlando knows her name, since he has never been told it in our hearing, but they are not likely to worry about it for long. The last few lines of the scene prepare for what is to come in Act II, scene iii, as well as for the scene immediately following, which is sometimes performed without a pause, though there are reasons against this (see below).

Act I, scene iii (134 lines; approx. 7 minutes)

The scene has a dramatic shape roughly similar to that of the preceding scene, though the component parts are of very different relative lengths. Again we start with essentially comic discontent and move into a sequence of intense drama, before finally emerging into a lyric playfulness. This scene – even the opening banter – has a generally darker tone, however.

    It seems likely that a few hours have passed, though it is possible we are in the same place as at the end of Act I, scene ii and no time at all has passed (as some productions have chosen to assume). An imagined change of place and a very brief pause between the scenes, however, seem more consistent with Rosalind's change of mood since the previous scene. The specific details of the locale may not matter, since it is not likely that it will be realistically represented on the stage, but it is none the less useful to think about how our awareness of locale functions in the scene. The action seems to occur not in a large public space, like the previous scene, but in a smaller, more confined, private place, perhaps Celia's or Rosalind's apartment in the ducal palace. It will probably be more effective if imagined as private living quarters (referred to in II.ii.5–7), into which Duke Frederick harshly intrudes. Perhaps the strongest argument for the locale being private is found in the last part of the scene. When the Duke has angrily departed, Rosalind and Celia behave as if they are in a place where they can express their feelings freely and plan their escape.

As in the preceding scene, both prose and verse are used, perhaps using the same criterion as before, namely, that prose is more appropriate in the lighter, wittier exchanges between Celia and Rosalind at the start of the scene, while verse is necessary to express the feelings Duke Frederick feels and arouses. After the Duke's departure, relatively serious verse continues to be used, since the problem he has created remains, but it shifts into a more lilting style when Celia broaches and Rosalind seizes upon the idea of disguise. From this point, there is a linguistic flow that continues to the cheerful rhymed couplet which ends the scene.

The imagery of the scene generally follows the pattern of its general form. The opening sequence between the two girls is notably full of plays on words and everyday imagery. The language shifts to a more elevated, almost biblical tone in the interaction with Duke Frederick. This is serious, direct emotional phrasing, with, surprisingly, a single brief touch of the classical in line 71.

The scene sums up and brings all the dramatic tensions of the play to a critical point, providing the impetus for what is to follow.

1–35   The scene begins with a variation on the opening of the preceding scene, though the feelings are developed more fully and the language is much stronger. Celia's jokes about Rosalind's love are a little sharp, perhaps because she fears she may be losing her friend. Rosalind is restless and her humour tart as she talks of her love. The shift from her earlier concern for her father to her present preoccupation with her 'child's father' provides an unexpected insight into the effect of love on parent–child bonds, perhaps even a suggestion of why she doesn't later bother to seek him out.

38–61   Falling in love with Orlando has shaken Rosalind, and Duke Frederick's brutal and unjust banishment adds to her turbulent state of mind. Her pleas on her own behalf are eloquent, revealing her intelligence, her courage and her deep-seated pride. For all her playfulness, she is an adult and genuinely serious person. This recognition provides an important underpinning to the subsequent development of the character.

102–34   It is an important aspect of the romantic yet theatrically comic nature of the play that characterization can change quickly. Thus, while the seriousness of Rosalind and Celia as they respond to banishment is entirely genuine, they end the scene like two children playing at dressing up to go, on their own, on an exciting trip to the country – perhaps even, if stage props are used, pulling clothes out of a chest to try on.

103   'My uncle' not 'your father'. Why? Does Celia perhaps have a fond memory of Duke Senior as a doting uncle? The audience may wonder why the suggestion does not come from Rosalind, though she is clearly more distraught than Celia. Later, they might wonder again why she does not try to find her father, and still later, when she finally does meet him, why doesn't she reveal her identity? Such questions are not raised explicitly. In Elizabethan comedy, logic does not play an important role in either narrative or character motivation (any more than it does in modern films). In practical terms, the reason Rosalind avoids her supposedly beloved father is that the plot (and the character) would not work if she had an active relationship with him. In romance, lovers have to be free to seek their beloved, who must either be absent or suffering from mistaken identity. Once the plot is under way, fathers are usually ignored unless they play an active role in bringing the lovers together or (more often) keeping them apart. In this respect, the characterization of Rosalind conforms to the conventions of traditional comedy.

107–24   Celia's brilliant suggestion revives Rosalind; she comes to life at last. Once again it is a game – and specifically a game of play-acting – that has stimulated her. The sequence provides the only instance of metatheatre in the scene. The moment dressing up is mentioned, these playful characters inevitably become performers, discussing what names to take, perhaps even rummaging out possible costumes. Rosalind's suggestion that they bring along the fool increases the possibility of more metatheatrical fun to come in the Forest of Arden. At this same point in the scene, the actors might well begin to play a little more directly to the audience, starting the metatheatrical game which will increasingly figure in the play. Rosalind's lines about men's cowardly braggadocio (115–18) provide an obvious opportunity to get a laugh, as they undoubtedly did when the Elizabethan boy actor played them openly to the audience.

133–4   The play is now firmly headed towards a happy ending, attention no longer focused on what fearful things may happen here or in banishment, but only on what exciting adventures 'liberty' will bring. Specifically, the last 31 lines of the scene start the movement towards Arden and the action that is to ensue. The last two lines, with the shift from 'banishment' to 'liberty,' epitomize the shift to an altogether new phase in the action.

ACT II

Act II, scene i (69 lines; approx. 4 minutes)

This scene takes the form of a symposium, or dinner conversation. A group of upper class gentlemen, wearing 'rustic' dress, sit around talking comfortably, more than likely finishing their drinks as they do so.

Seemingly, the play has entered the realm of the pastoral: the Forest of Arden, perhaps in winter (ll. 6–9). Specifically, the locale consists of a semi-civilized encampment, the forest 'court'of the banished Duke Senior, with a table, benches and so on. The existence of other particular places within the forest, which will be discovered in later scenes, is pointed to by the First Lord's description of Jaques's forest glade soliloquizings. This scene establishes a normative style on which the rest of the Arden scenes work variations. Under the benign aegis of the gentle Duke Senior, the action seems likely henceforth to avoid serious conflicts and have a gentler, more harmonious flow (to be interrupted only twice by brief, brutal appearances by Duke Frederick).

Accordingly, the acting here must be elegant, unaffected and well-spoken, as the status of the characters requires, but without becoming languid, since an audience, while enjoying the change of tone and situation, will not want the performance to lose momentum. It is of course the characters' enthusiasm for their subjects (life in the forest, Jaques) which carries the scene.

The language is verse: despite the rustic setting, these are not countrymen but displaced, well-educated gentlemen. The style is rather highflown and the images sometimes strained, as suits the characters' class and the idealized pastoral perspective.

1–17   The speech illustrates how differently thematic material is handled here. The subject of fraternal conflict and usurpation, which we have seen being aggressively enacted in the previous scenes, is here gently talked about from the perspective of the stoical victim. The comfortable situation of this 'country court' itself constitutes a rather soft statement of the theme of political power and the contrasts between court and country.

Duke Senior is quickly characterized as gracious and gentle, but also a bit pompous and with a strong moralistic bent. His thoughtful elegance of language and speech, together with his fondness for moralizing and his sentimental but intelligent interest in his surroundings, are what most clearly characterize him. The role is sometimes played by the same actor as Duke Frederick, in which case thought must be given to the necessary contrasts and how they can best be created. At the same time, there may be some slight resemblance between the two brothers. As the character of Duke Senior develops, we see a sharper side to him, such as his dislike of inferiors (for example, Jaques) disagreeing with him: see his comments on Jaques (II.vii.5–6) and Jaques's on him (II.v.31–2).

16–17   Arden is a locale with many meanings. From this point onwards in the play, locale has quite a different kind of function (see above, pp. 40–1).

29–66   The First Lord's storytelling performance to his captive audience is the one piece of metatheatre in the scene. He obviously enjoys his own performance, giving satirical renditions of Jaques's moralistic–melodramatic speeches, perhaps including a vocal imitation. This set-piece serves to introduce the highly theatrical character of Jaques.

47–57   Jaques's language, as quoted, breaks the pattern of the scene in being noticeably excessive, as if he were always trying to impress an audience. The emotionality of his observations and his critical comments on Duke Senior and his court make his language more colourful than that of the Duke and his Lords, whom we cannot imagine using such eccentric, hyperbolic language.

60–3   Jaques's ironic comment puts the theme of the unjust seizure of power in a surprising new context: supposed victims themselves becoming usurpers. This is our first indication of his perverseness and originality.

69   At the end of the scene, we are left in anticipation of meeting Jaques, who seems likely to provide considerable entertainment. Shakespeare has distracted us with this gentle scene, so we are emotionally unprepared for the shock that is to follow, though the return of the exiles back to the tyrant who sent them there is dramatically logical.

Act II, scene ii (21 lines; approx. 1 minute)

Again the world of serious drama, the angry, treacherous atmosphere of Duke Frederick's court. The scene is hysterical in tone and
tempo, both in the Duke's seething fury and in the barely suppressed
panic of the Lords. The particular location is unspecified and imma-
terial. Coming immediately after the benign atmosphere of the
preceding scene, the Duke's entrance seems almost a savage invasion
of the peaceful forest – as, much later, we hear he had set out to do
(see V.iv.153–7). The change of locale here provides a powerful and
vivid contrast between the two worlds of the play and the two ruling
personages. The immediate juxtaposition of the two dukes makes
their differences even more striking, especially if, as is sometimes
done, the same actor plays both roles.

The language is verse, but with an entirely different tone and
vocabulary from that of the preceding scene. Everything spoken here
has a specific practical purpose; the only emotions are anger and the
fear it provokes. The rhythm is on the whole sharp and rather irregular, particularly in the Duke's speeches. Perhaps most important of
all, it is fast – much different from the easy pace of the previous scene.

1–3   Now more isolated than ever, Duke Frederick has turned
deeply inward and become even more suspicious. Is he entirely para-
noid or could he be right? Has Le Beau perhaps given the fugitives
secret assistance? If so, the Duke's accusation might provoke some
visible reaction from him.

4–16   This is the only time there is an outside view of Rosalind and
Celia. The clear suggestion that Celia's 'gentlewoman' regularly
eavesdropped on her mistress and generated gossip about her are
consistent with the suspicious, treacherous atmosphere of Duke
Frederick's court.

17–21   The orders to capture not only Rosalind and Celia, but also
Orlando or his brother bring the two main actions of the play together.
At the same time, we are led into the next scene by the reference to
Orlando, as well as by the high state of emotional tension which carries

on into it. The continuing mood of imminent danger might also be prepared for by the use of intensely shadowed lighting here.

Act II, scene iii (76 lines; approx. 4 minutes)

A serious, highly dramatic scene, in which two of the play's most sympathetic characters, caught in a dangerous situation, struggle to find a way out. The basic action parallels what we have seen in Act I, scene iii: a heroic young character threatened with death by a villain and driven into exile, though Orlando's departure is given more extended and dramatic treatment than Rosalind's. His feeling is not playful like hers, but, after initial despair and uncertainty, resolute and determined. These differences express the contrast between the two characters, one playful and ironic (though with strong feelings), the other earnest and serious.

The scene is in verse, with a number of long, rhetorical speeches expressing a character's elaborated, highly emotional responses to a situation rather than addressing some immediate purpose.

1 The general locale is the same as in the play's first scene, though now we are not in the orchard but at the entrance to the house. (Some editors of the play have had Orlando knocking on the door to start the scene, though there is no stage direction about a door in the original text.) That this is a dangerous place is underlined in the opening lines, then further confirmed by the revelation of Oliver's murderous plot. Locale is therefore an immediate practical issue in the scene: this is a place where Orlando must not stay, though like Rosalind (I.iii.102) he still doesn't know where he can go. Orlando's first words suggest that the scene can be played in comparative darkness, which suits his apprehension about returning and Adam's fear for his safety. Two characters entering fearfully from different places, not seeing each other in the dark, can easily become comic, however, if not carefully staged and acted.

2–30 Adam's distressed response to Oliver's earlier mistreatment (I.i. 82–4) is amplified here. He begins the scene very distraught, his speech breathless and disconnected. It is striking how almost lyrical rhetorical questions are mixed with parent-like reprimands and complaints about the state of the world. As he goes on, his confusion increases, until by the end he is almost hysterical. Adam is shown more fully than before, revealing the depth of feeling that gives him such sympathy and authority. The character was much admired in the eighteenth and nineteenth centuries as a moral example, as well as (perhaps) because of a tradition – of which there is no tangible evidence – that it was played by Shakespeare.

3–4 At the start, we feel that this young man is with an old man who is a combination of surrogate father and faithful retainer. We can easily imagine Orlando as a boy being looked after by the faithful Adam. This theme is highlighted by Adam's 'O you memory of old Sir Rowland' (ll. 3–4). However, that their relationship is one of master and servant is repeatedly emphasized.

29–68 The character of Orlando is filled out considerably. At first, it is shown how he can fall into despairing hysteria. Then, when he has been comforted by old Adam, he displays his capacity for another kind of love. His response to the prospect of exile is like Rosalind's: both are at a loss at first, needing the practical suggestion of a confidant to spur them to action (compare I.iii.102–12 and II.iii.38–68). Once another person has given them an idea, they are revitalized and immediately seize the initiative.

56–65 Orlando's moral encomium on faithful servants expresses a concern, widespread at the time of the play, about the deterioration of the old values of family and service (see above, p. 9).

66–8 The comparatively cheerful departure into exile echoes the ending of Act I, scene iii, a parallel underlined by the use of the word 'content'.

69–76 Adam's farewell epilogue, with its careful rhyming couplets, gives the scene's ending the formality of a moral fable or folk tale. As old Adam trudges wearily off, the audience is prepared to see Rosalind, Celia and Touchstone trudge wearily on.

Act II, scene iv (98 lines; approx. 5 minutes)

A little over a quarter of the way through the play (750 lines out of 2722), we have reached what would be the beginning of the second act if the play were in the modern three-act form. As might be expected, the scene is about a new beginning in a new place, meeting new characters.

With the arrival in Arden, the play moves into a more metatheatrical mode. This is instigated by the actors appearing in new costumes, another reminder that all this is a game of make-believe. In their new setting and attire, the three main characters of the scene, now freed from the constraints of the court, start to develop new personalities. With a new persona overlaid onto the original character, each becomes a double character, offering opportunities for each actor to play her/his new persona against the original one. A reflection of this doubling is found in the scene's language, which is a mixture of prose and verse, another indication of how flexibly the two are intermingled throughout the play.

The scene deals with two of the play's main themes: romantic love and court versus country, which are of course interwoven throughout. The brevity of each action unit emphasizes that this scene is a transitional one: both we and the characters are moving through the plot and through the forest.

1 The scene's opening is virtually farcical, as Rosalind and Celia trudge wearily onto the stage, Touchstone staggering after them with their baggage. Each comments on her/his condition in a characteristic way. As they appear, we immediately register their new costumes, including Touchstone's (presumably), though there has been some dispute about what he may have worn in the original staging. 'Alias' in the original text suggests that he too may have chosen to put on a 'disguise'. The changes of costume reinforce the sense almost of a new play beginning, with a new locale and new expectations about the characters.

1–16 The characters are somewhat altered. Rosalind is now released (perhaps by her assumed masculinity, which is here underlined) into that confident playfulness which primarily defines the role. There is the opportunity for the actor to perform feelings and ideas, both to her fellow actors and to the audience, more flexibly and independently. From this point onwards, the character becomes more fully expressed, displaying the irony that is central to the role, even when she acknowledges her passion for Orlando. She and Celia are no longer the kind of equals they were earlier. One reason is Rosalind's new masculinity, which gives her more authority when they meet new people. Another reason is that the play now becomes focused on her life, not Celia's. From this point onwards, Celia takes on a different role, as confidante, ironic commentator and – quite importantly – metatheatrical surrogate spectator. Touchstone's new role shows him less dependent on Rosalind and Celia, now a much larger frog in the smaller pond of Arden, engaged in developing relationships with the inhabitants of this new country. Interestingly for the actor, the character is no longer confined to the limited status of professional court jester and can begin to play the roles of visiting courtier, authoritative satirical commentator and, eventually, lover. In accordance with all this, the actors may well enter with a strong awareness of playing new roles, very slightly exaggerating the obvious traits they now exhibit on this new 'stage': a young man bravely escorting a young lady in distress, the pathetically distressed young lady herself, and the clown making the most of his enforced porter's role. Especially important is the movement change in the actor playing Rosalind/'Ganymede', whose new masculine costume will presumably permit and encourage greater freedom and exuberance. An idea of how she might move in her new role has already been suggested by the satirical swagger demonstrated at I.iii.113–18, though it will certainly be adapted and modified as her new circumstances reveal themselves.

8   The line may be intended to prepare and justify Celia's reduced importance in this scene and the ones following.

12–15   Rosalind's formal declaration, the first naming of the locale since I.i.114, allows Touchstone another opportunity for a metatheatrical joke with a play on the two meanings of 'fool'.

17–18 The change to a new, more metatheatrical setting is suggested by the formal introduction of these two new characters, almost in the manner of an old prologue. With this entrance, we are told that we are in a different *kind* of place, a new, almost artificial-seeming 'country' – a fiction within a fiction – which proves to be the land of the pastoral and at the same time the simple countryside. An interesting feature of the presentation of this new land on stage is that a particular locality within it will often provide more than one acting space. This might be based on one of the associations of 'forest', that the trees afford ready concealment, though it is most likely to be a simple exploitation of the nature of the Elizabethan public theatre stage and a means of establishing and emphasizing the increased metatheatricality, which is helped by characters being able simultaneously to occupy different parts of the acting area, observing and listening to others.

Finally, the almost formal introduction of Corin and Silvius emphasizes the half-literary, half-metatheatrical artificiality of their exchange, considerably increased of course by Silvius's histrionic performance.

18–42 The verse here is clearly meant to be an appropriate language for the conventional pastoral shepherd in love, but is obviously parodic. This passage introduces the romantic love of the pastoral in a very satirical way, a sharply different treatment from that so far given the love of Rosalind and Orlando.

43–54 This little set-piece serves two purposes in the development of Touchstone: it establishes his satirical attitude towards the country and prepares us for his discovery of a successor to Jane Smile in Audrey. It also adds another couple to the series of lover-pairings presented in the space of a minute: this is the third, and each one is different. It might also provide the actor with a chance to try out a mocking imitation of Silvius. Rosalind's tolerant and ironic response is a lovely character touch.

62 This is the first instance of Touchstone's assumption of the role of courtly sophisticate condescending to uncouth country folk, which continues for the rest of the play. Here he affects a ridiculous posh accent and, perhaps, something like a loud 'public school prefect' voice. This can be the start of the actor of the part developing a new forest persona for himself, which he demonstrates in his interplay with Corin, and later, Audrey, William and Sir Oliver Martext.

67–98   The return to verse shows Rosalind's courtesy to Corin, beginning an exchange which is friendly and polite on both sides, yet rather formal. We are reminded of the class difference between them. In paying him the courtesy of addressing him in verse, she subtly underlines Corin's high moral status as a man of virtue, whose directness and simplicity remind us of Adam (providing another link between the two lovers). The shift from prose also gives dignity to the idealized presentation of the countryside so characteristic of pastoral romance, which is here given additional strength by the practical dealings with Corin. Far from lowering the romantic tone, such down-to-earth detail gently makes the pastoral fantasy more real: we are encouraged to imagine not only visiting paradise but being able to settle into a charming, affordable cottage there.

   Rosalind here for the first time plays the role of 'Ganymede', in this case a polite young gentleman, as Corin immediately recognizes. There are several other 'Ganymedes' to come, varying considerably with who she is dealing with. This is her first attempt at the new role, and she is surely enjoying it, as she may indicate in little looks exchanged with Celia.

Act II, scene v (59 lines; approx. 3 minutes)

More of the leisurely life of the forest courtiers, this time in the form of an interlude, an openly theatrical entertainment with no significant dramatic content. The players are in the same general locale as in Act II, scene i, a part of the Forest as a 'sylvan' rather than a 'rural' place, where the main occupations for those of higher class and concerns are eating, drinking, singing and hunting. It is again a setting for metatheatricality, though this time of a different kind. The scenes involving Duke Senior's pastoral court provide what might be called a sort of background mood music (actually and metaphorically) to the main action. There is, however, one slightly sour note: Jaques and his satirical melancholy. The most striking thing about these scenes is the complete absence of any strong dramatic motivation. Unlike the other characters in the play, those in Duke Senior's court have everything they want, are involved in no emotional relationships and show no desire to change their lives.

1–8, 35–42 The song is a celebration by the forest courtiers of the relaxed and simple life they enjoy, in contrast to the harassed, artificial existence at court. Though it can be arranged otherwise, the text assumes that the four-line verses are sung by Amiens, with the other courtiers joining in the lyrical refrains.

9 Jaques's demand – if he means more singing, not more drink – raises the question of the status of Amiens. While he performs the function of something like court musician, he is a gentleman, not a servant, perhaps a relative of Duke Senior, who calls him 'cousin' (II.vii.173). For the actor of the role, then, both the ability to sing and the style to play a courtly gentleman are necessary.

22–6 Has Jaques been drinking? His conduct in the scene and this speech in particular make him seem like a sad, sour drunk. His comments on 'thank-yous' are as bitter as any he utters in the play.

29–34 Jaques's relationship to the Duke is a little anomalous. Though an educated gentleman, he plays the part of jester at the forest court. As an upper-class clown, he adopts the character of a melancholic (the sad-faced clown is a historically recurring type), while showing the independent spirit of both jester and gentleman by making critical comments about his superiors, as we have heard Touchstone doing in an earlier scene (I.ii.75–81). His language is sometimes a more educated version of Touchstone's earthy clownish wordplay (compare, for example, II.v.12–26 with I.ii. 67–74). He also shares Touchstone's liking for the formalities of dispute, though he is fonder of real argument than the clown and doesn't like to be disagreed with. For the actor, Jaques provides the opportunity to play not only whimsical eccentricity but also a bit of self-approving acidity: as Alan

Rickman, who played the role in 1985, put it, 'He's very sure of himself and a bit of a mess' (*Players of Shakespeare* 2, 1988, p. 75).

43–54   With false diffidence, Jaques presents his own sour version of the carefree verses that we have heard, simply inverting the pleasant things in the original to create a satirical commentary representing his own 'melancholic' – actually misanthropic – view. The actor may choose to sing it or recite it: if the former, in a suitably unmusical style.

57–9   His last lines sustain the impression that Jaques is a bit drunk: the explanation of 'ducdame' is a dismissive, off-the-cuff invention and the desire to sleep entirely expectable, though the wry and whimsical addition of the 'first-born of Egypt' shows his mind still working in its own inspired and peculiar way. The casual exits here provide a nice ironic prelude to Orlando and Adam, desperately struggling through this very same forest in the next scene.

Act II, scene vi (18 lines; approx. 1 minute)

This short scene carries on the action from Orlando and Adam's last scene together (II.iii), though of course in a new place, and serves the purpose of moving the Orlando plot another step towards the connection with Rosalind. The action is still in the Forest of Arden, but in a very different part – for the first time, one that is felt to be full of hardship and danger. For one of only two occasions in the play (the other being IV.iii), it becomes more than a playground, its metatheatrical function suspended.

The scene is in very simple and direct prose, without rhetorical amplification, and strikingly different from that of their earlier scene; this is partly accounted for, of course, by their state of exhaustion. This is one of the play's simplest and most intimate passages, romantic in the sense of focusing on feeling above all. The positive theme of affection and loyalty between servant and master is again illustrated.

1   The treatment of the arrival of these two characters in the forest is yet another example of subtle, continuing parallels between

Rosalind's and Orlando's situations and responses. Both this arrival and Rosalind's in Act II, scene iv, show the leading characters protecting others. The beginnings of Act I, scenes i and ii, and their similar reactions to adversity and departures into exile in Act I, scene iii, and Act II, scene iii, can also be compared. We have just seen the food old Adam is dying for laid out at the end of the preceding scene, and it is about to reappear in the following scene – unless the staging chooses to keep it ironically visible throughout this scene.

1–3 Adam is now crushed by old age and hardship, unable to live up to his earlier assurances that he is 'strong and lusty' (II.iii.47). Though he is at the end of his strength, he is as selfless as ever. The task of the actor remains the same: not to let the character become too sentimentalized.

4–18 Orlando's emotional resilience and kindness are seen again. Like Rosalind, he is strong in adversity. His goodness to Adam is made even more touching by his gentle humour as he comforts the old man, the first indication we have had that he has a sense of humour, something that will be called upon in the later scenes with 'Ganymede'. This element in Orlando's character is a useful antidote to his earnest besottedness with Rosalind, giving, perhaps, a sign of the man he will become when he has outgrown the adolescence of love.

Act II, scene vii (203 lines; approx. 10 minutes)

The very different feelings experienced in this part of the Forest from those in the one we have just seen underlines the emotional fluidity that this multi-locale gives to the play. The banquet that was being prepared is ready and the characters now sit down and eat it, while of course they go on talking. The scene thus becomes another symposium, with Jaques the star performer. It seems almost incidental when, towards the close of the scene, Orlando's and Adam's desperate flight comes to a safe end.

The scene is in verse, aside from a few lines of prose, which are barely noticeable, since the verse (except for some parts of the long set-pieces) has such a vernacular flavour and flow. The contrasts between different characters are set out in their language: the serious sententiousness of the Duke, the impulsive yet well-mannered style of Orlando and, above all, the highly flavoured verse of Jaques, who has his own unique vocabulary and way of speaking. The scene offers perhaps the richest and most entertaining verse of the play, though hardly rivalling Rosalind's prose in other scenes.

Despite a considerable amount of moralizing by both Duke Senior and Jaques, the main themes of the play are only indirectly touched upon. The locale is less a model of the pastoral life as romantic ideal than it is an ironic setting for Jaques's disillusioned performances.

1–4 The scene's action carries on, after a brief passage of time, from the endings of Act II, scenes v and vi, bringing together the characters from those scenes. Duke Senior went off at the end of Act II, scene i, to find Jaques; at the end of Act II, scene v, Amiens went to fetch the Duke; at the end of Act II, scene vi, Orlando went off to find food. Now the Duke, still wondering where Jaques is, has grown impatient and a little irritable. In this way, the scene is set up for the arrival of Jaques at the forest court, which has been delayed since Act II, scene i. When he arrives, he dominates the stage, speaking 99 of the 203 lines in the scene.

5–6 The old Duke's character is developed considerably in this scene, as he begins to show a little more sharpness towards Jaques, partly – but surely not entirely – because he has had to chase him through the forest. His attitude towards his court jester is ambivalent.

12–61 Playing to his natural audience, Jaques is more fully revealed. Though he claims to be a melancholic, he is much more. His sporadic melancholy is an adopted and self-conscious pose, essentially comic, more a style of performing himself than a real set of mind. He knows that the role of melancholic makes him a kind of fool to others, providing them with entertainment, but at the same time it gives him a loftier position, safer from ridicule. In this scene it becomes clear that his main talent is as a high-comedy clown delivering sour performances for his patron. He is a perpetual performer whose self-importance drives him to seek the limelight whenever possible: when he is on the stage, he seeks to be the dominant person. As one critic has put it: 'The party was never complete when he wasn't there, and never at ease when he was' (Thomson, 1974, p. 150).

The actor of this role has the opportunity to play several elements of the character against each other: his vanity, his wit, his sensitivity to criticism (as seen in his later prickly relationships with 'Ganymede' and Orlando) and his considerable charm. The description of meeting Touchstone echoes a previous account of finding an eccentric in the forest, the First Lord's in Act II, scene i. Jaques's very stagey entrance is further evidence that he is, above all, a self-conscious performer. His histrionic repetitions of 'fool' and the extended set-piece on the subject of fools are examples of a character metatheatrically playing actor, performing in this case to an audience of the Duke and his fellow courtiers, but also of course to the theatre audience as well. It is as an actor that he speaks Touchstone's own words in the laughable monologues about Lady Fortune (see Rosalind and Celia's exchanges in I.ii) and on the subject of time (see Rosalind on the same subject in III.ii.294–327). At the same time, both these speeches sound rather like a parody of Jaques's own way of speaking: certainly lines 26–8 foreshadow Jaques's own Ages of Man in lines 139–66.

14 The first part of the line might provide a cue for everyone, led by Jaques, to sit down and begin eating, though Jaques, if he does sit, will probably pop up again to continue his performance.

37–8 He may be quoting Touchstone. The line could imply 'gift' not only as intelligence but as material payment for their beauty.

43 The Duke ironically confirms not only Jaques's character but his semi-official position at the forest court.

62–9 He has begun to weary of Jaques's self-importance, as he has already shown by his change from addressing him with the friendly 'you' at the start (ll. 10–11) to calling him 'thou', a form used to inferiors and servants, in line 44 and here. Finally, he rebukes Jaques sharply for his unsavoury past, directing against him an accusation commonly directed against satirists.

70–87   Jaques defends the satirist's function in a manner associated with well-known satirical writers of the time (for example, Ben Jonson). Shakespeare may be using Jaques here to present a defence of satire, which was under attack at the time of the play's first appearance.

88–119   The entrance is a startling interruption of a flowing comic performance by a very different character with a very different emotional agenda. Orlando is again in his impulsive, potentially violent mood, though he at first excuses his rudeness on the grounds of his distress. Pressed further by a second reprimand from Duke Senior, he claims he was only pretending to be fierce. What is striking is how strongly and protractedly he insists he is a gentleman, this being a sore point with him, as we have seen from the first moments of the play. The Duke picks up on Orlando's claim to be a gentleman, but adds the second sense of 'gentle', as meaning kindly and polite. The second meaning, especially here, seems clearly dependent on the first, however, and we are finally left with the impression that the primary criterion of good behaviour in this situation is that it should be upper class. The actor playing Orlando will have to deal with two problems: a seeming over-concern about breeding, in the middle of a critical situation, and coming forward with the main argument for giving him help – the plight of poor starving Adam – only after he has gone through two assertions of his social status and a long, rather rhetorical speech about the good life he and the Duke's forest court have lost.

89, 91, 101   Jaques's annoyance at being interrupted in the middle of a performance is considerable. In one production, he calmly walked to the table at line 101 and, in defiance of Orlando's threat, took a bite of an apple. His ill-tempered remarks perhaps lay the groundwork of the enmity between the two which we see later (III.ii.247–89).

136–66   Another of Duke Senior's characteristic commonplaces, this is an obvious cue for Jaques's famous Seven Ages of Man speech (ll. 139–66). He may well have prepared this metatheatrical performance piece in advance, in which case it will have a very practised air about it. As we expect, he takes the stage and plays it to the full, floating around the table and perhaps even at some point(s) using it as an acting platform. The actor may choose to perform each of the types as he describes them, though he will probably prefer only to suggest them rather than act them out literally. The speech is theatrical not only in its delivery and rhetorical structuring, but also in the series of types it sets forth, most of whom (particularly the lover, the soldier, the justice, and the old man) are familiar characters from traditional comedy. The entrance of old Adam – exhausted, weak and starving, carried (or at least supported) by Orlando – just as Jaques describes the seventh age, may be thought too illustrative in the wrong way. An alternative would be for Jaques to finish his speech, with enthusiastic applause from the Duke and Lords – which evokes his sickliest smirk – followed by the entrance, which has an immediate sobering effect on the company.

169–70   This is Adam's last appearance, though some productions have brought him on in the last scene of the play as a benign presence at the weddings. In the original staging, the actor playing the role may have been needed for doubling, perhaps as Sir Oliver Martext or even (it is perfectly feasible) as Corin. Dramatically, there is nothing more for the character to do, now that he has completed his function of accompanying Orlando to safety. Some might argue that Jaques's description of old age, despite its seeming inappropriateness, intimates Adam's death.

173–93   Another metatheatrical reminder, following Jaques's set-pieces, that we are watching a theatrical performance. The mood of the song suits the pathetic spectacle of old Adam, and the words recall the bitterness caused by the ingratitude of cruel masters like Oliver to faithful servants. There may also be a faint intimation that all those of the forest court, including the Duke himself, live with some underlying bitterness at the injustice of the cruel world which has exiled them. One such story of injustice is being whispered to the Duke by Orlando as they sit at the table during the song.

198–203   The Duke performs his almost ceremonial function by bringing the scene to a quite formal conclusion. His speech gathers the strands of the story together, the final line leading our minds back to the court of Duke Frederick.

ACT III

Act III, scene i (18 lines; approx. 1 minute)

The last appearance of Duke Frederick and the final step in the gradual intensification of the dark and dynamic style associated with his and Oliver's villainy. For the first and only time, the play's two villains are seen together, the Duke completely dominant. The locale of the scene might almost be described as Duke Frederick's raging mind: a modern production might for that reason choose to light the scene expressionistically, producing sharply shadowed faces. The action is reduced to an irrational monologue, performed in a style which is the most savage in the play. The language is a jagged and brutal verse, with uneven rhythms and unexpected shifts of syntax, a complete contrast to the verse of the foregoing and following scenes.

This is the fifth banishment in the play (including those of Duke Senior, Rosalind, Celia and Orlando), the darkest point in the development of the theme of brotherly rivalries, and it reverberates as a haunting memory through later scenes, notably in Oliver's narration in Act IV, scene iii. The scene's ending points us back to Orlando's story, which resumes after this interruption.

13–14   Oliver is in a very different position from when we last saw him. For the first time, he is a victim not an oppressor and his pleading speech shows no trace of his former arrogance. Is it possible that this new situation, together with the irrational savagery of Duke Frederick's anger, might lead him to begin questioning his own feelings and conduct towards his brother? Seeing him as a victim might soften the audience slightly towards him, in preparation for the later transformation.

15   The Duke's comment on Oliver's pathetic protest echoes the abruptness with which he dismissed Celia's affirmation of her loyalty to Rosalind (I.iii.83), as well as being an ironic comment on his own behaviour.

18   The Duke turns and strides off. The lords stand silent for a moment, stunned by his rage, before grimly escorting Oliver away. He has been destroyed. His face and body during this pause might speak of what has happened to him – perhaps even suggest that it might change him.

Act III, scene ii (441 lines; approx. 21 minutes)

Almost the midpoint of the play. A sudden shift from the murderous madness of Duke Frederick to the lighter love-madness of Orlando. The two main characters, Rosalind and Orlando, are finally reunited, but with a twist. The locale has changed to yet another part of the Forest of Arden, neither the hospitable rural locale first discovered by Rosalind and Celia, nor the comfortable camp where the old Duke and his gentle courtiers live and sing, eat and drink. The Forest is now obviously a place where people wander freely and come upon each other unexpectedly. The play has moved nearer to the Forest's heart, for Orlando's poems on the trees transform it into an emblem of the romantic state of mind. With the exception of two brief passages, the scene is devoted to the play's main theme of love. It is in the playful irony of this scene that the main tone of the play's treatment of this theme is established. The gentle mockery of love by the lover her(and him)self is an essential part of the play's statement about love as both a human folly and a strength.

The predominant language is the vivacious and flexible prose which distinguishes this play above all others of Shakespeare's. It is full of invention and surprising figures of speech, mingling many commonplace expressions and literary extracts. At the same time, it never ceases to be the language of people speaking, as opposed to people making speeches (except of course when the speeches are mainly parodic and/or performative, as with Jaques or Touchstone). One element contributing to this quality is the structuring of much of the scene as a series of metatheatrical exchanges between characters observed by other characters as onstage spectators: in a sense, characters performing for each other and thus more readily – on occasion – to the audience.

The scene is the longest in the play, in itself a virtual one-act play, in the course of which we see a clearly developed progression, interspersed with brief delaying scenes.

1   A sudden, sharp contrast with the previous scene: Orlando drifts onto the stage in a virtual ecstasy of love, gently hanging the paper on the tree as if it were some sacred object. The action is a declaration not only of his love but also of the foolish extremity to which it has now come: the audience may remember how different his behaviour was when he was first smitten (for example, I.ii.239–41) and think he has changed for the worse.

10   The exit is like that of Silvius at II.iv.40.

11–83   They stroll on from another direction, having a friendly chat, which becomes an extended comic set-piece on the subject of country versus court life, performed by two familiar kinds of comic figures: the country bumpkin (of which Corin is a more sensible version) being interrogated by the know-it-all clown. The character of Corin is more fully developed here. His responses to Touchstone's derision demonstrate how much dignity and intelligence he possesses. He emerges from the exchange as worthy not simply of condescending sympathy but of respect.

This is one of the scenes of which Touchstone sees himself as the star. The actor may choose to play it like a quiet sage philosopher, strolling about as he ruminates, or he may want to combine the pompous philosophical disquisitions with a good deal of dance-like movement, not necessarily always appropriate to the words. Several basic comic movement routines might come into play here, for example:

1. The Back-and-forth Pro-and-con Yes-and-no Contradiction Dance (ll. 13–21), which has two persons – Touchstone 1 and Touchstone 2 – played in rapid sequence by the same dancer (Touchstone), each delivering his argument to the other with a suitable gesture.
2. The Idle-curiosity-approach-to-damnation Dance (ll. 31–7), in which he sidles up to Corin with a seemingly-casual question, then hops–wheels around and confronts him full-frontally with the threat of damnation.
3. The Back-and-forth Rebuttal Dance (ll. 39–67), which involves moving close to his opponent, making a firm demand, then taking the reply and making a half-skipping little tour before coming back with the next demand.
4. The Final Closure Dance (ll. 69–83), which begins with firm closure with the partner, perhaps actually embracing him, then progresses to an overwhelming, crescendo listing of the partner's disgusting 'sins', accompanied by suitable squeezings and arm-wavings.

(All of these are of course optional, depending on the actor's wishes and repertoire.) Another, simpler way of choreographing the sequence in broad spatial terms is suggested by the conventional question-and-answer format it employs: playing the courtroom prosecutor, Touchstone circles the hapless defendant (who calmly holds his ground) in a self-important stride, sometimes 'playing to the jury' (that is, the audience) when the responses obviously betray the simple-minded defendant's quite absurd ignorance, at other times bearing down upon him in a bullying way. A third option is for Touchstone to play the sequence ironically, that is, as a quiet, almost immobile conversation between two simple, honest souls, in a manner which parodies Corin's own serious placidity.

84–5 The lines suggest either that Rosalind does not see Corin and Touchstone as she enters or that they deliberately step aside and listen as she reads the poem: in either case, it is another little piece of metatheatre, the first of a succession of such sequences in this scene.

86–93, 97   Rosalind's performance is satirical and bound to be rather exaggerated, given the poem's doggerel rhythm and the absurd rhyme of 'Rosalind' (pronounced 'Rosa-lined'), which make it fair game for Touchstone. Her annoyance at his ridicule, however, makes it clear that her own mockery has had an undercurrent of affection – after all, she is herself the subject of the poem.

122–55   Another bit of metatheatre, though less comic perhaps, since this poem is much better than the one Rosalind has performed. Accordingly, Celia's reading is a more feeling rendition, which may be one reason why she is a bit unpleasantly surprised at having been overheard. To think that she may have been a bit moved by the poem might alleviate the notion that Celia is always the ironic, practical one, as well as subtly preparing for her later romantic susceptibility to Oliver.

160–247   This sequence is reminiscent of the opening of Act I, scene ii, where we first saw the two in playful conversation. Here the freedom and exuberance of spirits and language are far greater, however, showing yet again how these knowing young women maintain a double perspective on the events of the story: enormous enthusiasm and playful irony. The exchanges between them are not particularly feminine in the conventional or sentimental sense, but rather displays of the playful exuberance of two young adolescents. In other words, they are not feminine in the sense of being like the conventional male expectation of female or 'ladylike' behaviour. Instead, they show the kind of freedom more commonly associated (in the traditional view) with boys than girls – in fact, it is to be associated with adolescents of either sex. For the actors of Rosalind and Celia, exploring the play of young adolescents is a good way of understanding the characters and finding the most effective style of playing them. This exchange is one of the most delightful displays of youthful friendship we could hope to find in drama.

Rosalind's exemplary perspective on love takes the form of two contrasting modes of behaviour. One, her 'female' loving response, is confined to her scenes as Rosalind alone with Celia, or asides to her in other scenes. Even in these, her love is not entirely foolish. She is aware of the excessiveness of her behaviour (for example, in ll. 215–20), which gives it an entirely different flavour and emotional weight. The second mode is satirical and occurs mainly when she is playing 'Ganymede'. It is shown here in the satirical comments on the poems and later in her mockery of Orlando. This mode too, however, has frequent and ironic undercurrents of infatuation (as, for example, in ll. 173–5).

173 Whether in England or northern France, the real Forest of Arden would be unlikely to have had palm trees. Like the later olive trees (IV.iii.77), this is a purely literary arboreal species, perhaps meant to add an exotic touch to the story.

248–89 Another piece of metatheatre with onstage spectators. Like the earlier sequence with Touchstone and Corin, this is a theatrical set-piece in the form of a neat series of give-and-takes in which two familiar types ('Signor Love' and 'Monsieur Melancholy') engage in a mutually satirical encounter. The characters carry on from their unfriendly first meeting in Act II, scene vii, showing the natural antipathy of two very different kinds of romantics, the enthusiastic young lover and the jaded melancholic. Orlando may several times try to break off the conversation and start to exit (for example, after ll. 254, 258, 263, 279), but is stopped by a new attempt by Jaques to score a point. The exchange finally deteriorates into ill-natured name-calling as they part company and head off in different directions.

The exchange tells us more about both characters. An element of worldly sophistication is added to Orlando's character, while he also reveals that he can be pretty unpleasant when someone rubs him up the wrong way, as Jaques obviously does. It is not simply that he defends his love against Jaques's derision, but also that he just seems to find Jaques boring and annoying. This throws a useful sidelight on the characterization of Jaques, who is quite skilled at getting on people's nerves – not always intentionally. He has continued playing the role of melancholic misanthrope, relying on the people he talks to for confirmation and self-confidence. This doesn't work with Orlando, who is a very uncooperative interlocutor and sharply rebuffs Jaques's attempt to win him over to his kind of role-playing (ll. 272–4).

290–422   In this first of the play's two great love scenes, the pattern of onstage metatheatre continues. One effect is to heighten the audience's awareness of role-playing, as Rosalind expressly sets out to play the role of 'knave' and 'saucy lackey'. It is in this sequence that she for the first time plays to the hilt the performing opportunity offered by her adopted disguise, displaying her knowledge and wit in a brilliant bout of love play. The scene is dominated by the metatheatre of Rosalind's performance. The combination of boyishness and femininity is brilliantly acted out, but what is especially effective is the strain of playful irony running through it all. To a considerable extent, this was enhanced by the role having been written to be performed by a boy player, a fact generally implicit in the text. Modern audiences can often miss this, but it remains important, for it affects both the characterization and the actor's performance. The most obvious piece of role-playing, the adoption of the identity of 'Ganymede', is rendered even more metatheatrical by the different layers of disguise in play. There is Actor 1 playing a woman (Rosalind 1) playing a boy ('Ganymede'), who will later become Actor 2 playing a woman (Rosalind 2), who is an imaginary and ironic version of the first female role. The matter becomes even more complicated when we recognize that the 'Ganymede' who plays with Orlando is quite a different character from the 'Ganymede' who appears in later scenes with Silvius and Phebe. All these entertaining masquerades provide perpetual reminders that we are watching a clever comic actor at work. The metatheatre of this role-playing is the core of the specifically theatrical experience of *As You Like It*, the 'touchstone' on which the other dramatic and thematic elements are tested.

Rosalind's declaration that she intends to 'play the knave' like 'a saucy lackey' is appropriate to the action that follows, which is clearly the successful attempt to seduce Orlando to accept her as his make-believe lover. With this in mind, there are different ways of approaching the scene's physical movement. One might involve 'Ganymede' taking an early opportunity of lying on the grass (or a nearby 'rock' or 'log'?), tempting Orlando to come and sit by her, as he soon does. This would bring the two close to each other, leading to a sort of relaxed physical intimacy between them as they lounged together. The question of Orlando's feelings about this boy who looks like Rosalind would have to be thought out by the actors: it would be counterproductive to be misled by his 'pretty youth' (l. 328) into suggesting anything homoerotic. One obvious consequence of the double disguise of the boy player is that the sexuality of Rosalind's and Orlando's love is sublimated. Their lovemaking is mediated: whenever both characters express the extremities of their love, it is not directly to their beloved, but indirectly through another character of their own sex – 'Ganymede' in one case, Celia in the other.

Another choreographic option would involve 'Ganymede', carried away by the excitement of the situation, turning the exchange into a virtual dance of delight, moving around him teasingly, alternately approaching him suddenly with a cheeky remark (for example, at l. 359), then whirling away in the exuberance of her display of wit. The movement pattern here would be predominantly circular, as the stage of the Elizabethan theatre encouraged, and which is generally very suitable to comedy. (John Bowen, who played Orlando in 1985, comments that his director Terry Hands's 'simple solution to lovers' games was circles', adding, 'If you had a map of our footprints in the two major scenes of the second half, you would have a picture of spirals all over the stage (*Players of Shakespeare 1*, 1985, p. 73).) It might be added that since circular movement is subtly evocative of animal (and female) movement, it might be particularly appropriate here. However the movement is handled, Rosalind is all the while also performing to Celia, perhaps leaning against a nearby tree, as her sympathetic spectator. Importantly, this sequence offers the opportunity for the actor of Rosalind to play at the same time to the theatre audience. This option is available to the actor of the role throughout the whole latter part of the play (that is, in all the 'Ganymede' scenes), adding another dimension to the performance which can contribute additional enjoyment for the audience as the actor openly shares with them her/his pleasure in ironic play-acting.

The verbal content of the whole sequence is built on the now familiar comic pattern of one character displaying her skill by outwitting another, whose task is to play straight man, providing feeder lines or questions. The rhetorical sequence occurs in five clearly defined segments, tracing a development from a conventional opening conversation gambit through a series of anecdotal exchanges about love, in which s/he seduces him into more and more intimate engagement. When s/he has warmed him up (especially by the performance of a woman's foibles in lines 397–409) s/he delivers the masterstroke: the proposal that Orlando should let 'him' pretend to be his 'Rosalind'. Quite apart from welcoming the opportunity to be 'with' his beloved, he has already begun to incline towards 'Ganymede' in a way which stirs his feeling memory of Rosalind, which makes him that much readier for the game. Asking 'Ganymede' where s/he lives is another move towards intimacy, letting 'Ganymede' lead 'his' victim – now properly tamed – off to the cottage, only at the last moment remembering to turn and call out to Celia to follow. Having watched all of this with a mixture of surprised admiration, hysterical amusement and intimations of sadness at the prospect of losing her dear friend, Celia goes slowly after them, whereupon – as 'Ganymede' leads off a compliant Orlando – Touchstone leads on an obliging Audrey.

302–27   For an interesting comparison of this speech with Jaques's Ages of Man piece, see Jay Halio's comments quoted on pp. 152–3 below.

328   Orlando's immediate liking for this forest 'youth' is comparable to his first impulsive response to Rosalind – of whom 'Ganymede' reminds him (see V.iv.28–9) – and creates a connection between Rosalind's two identities which underpins the deception she is about to develop more fully. This marks the beginning not only of Orlando's susceptibility to deception (and self-deception), but also of the learning process through which she leads him. Another, crucially important aspect of Orlando's character is developed in this scene. In earlier scenes, with the exception of a brief and important passage in Act I, scene ii, we have seen his impulsiveness, his courage and his temper. Here his natural liking for 'Ganymede' – abetted by seeing an almost fraternal resemblance to Rosalind (see V.iv.28–9) – helps us understand him better, as well as giving an additional subtextual dimension to his relationship with Rosalind. Most revealing perhaps is his attitude towards his own lovesickness. He doesn't want to be cured of his love, of course, but he acknowledges that he is an 'unfortunate' victim of a malady and may actually be in need of 'curing'. At the same time, he openly enjoys being in love and can see himself as foolish without denying his feelings. This duality of attitude gives the character greater depth. None the less, what is central to the scene and to the later development of their relationship is his naivity in matters of love. For all his virtues, he is still a callow youth with much to learn about himself, love, and the world. Rosalind begins the process of educating him.

423   At the end, the audience is left looking forward to more interaction between Orlando and Rosalind as 'Ganymede', but they have learned by now that they will have to wait, that the play's style of construction doesn't allow an immediate continuation of the same action. The next meeting of the two lovers is withheld until three scenes (about 15 minutes) have passed.

Act III, scene iii (98 lines; approx. 5 minutes)

This scene provides a contrasting interlude dealing with the love theme in the form of low comic satire, and starting the small and entertaining subplot of Touchstone's courtship of Audrey. The language is low comic prose, Touchstone's long-winded affectation and bawdiness nicely counterpointed by the brevity and simplicity of Audrey's responses.

1–41   Audrey is a comic figure, of course, but not necessarily as farcical as some productions, perhaps seeking easy laughs, have made her. She seems more than a mere country clown, for while her ignorance is comic, it is complemented by good sense and real innocence. If she is played purely farcically, she becomes nothing more than a crude sexual object, a butt for Touchstone's jokes. If played as a comic character – that is, someone one who gets through to him – then there can be a more interesting interplay between them. One measure of her character can be found in Touchstone's treatment of her and how an audience might react to it. Though he condescends to her in this scene, of course, he still wants to marry her (for whatever reasons) and it seems clear later (V.i, V.iii) that he becomes actually fond of her, which gives her greater interest than she would have as a simple clown. For these reasons, the actor of Audrey might do well to avoid playing the role too broadly and limit herself to smaller farcical touches. The question of whether the actor of Audrey should acknowledge the audience's presence is a difficult one. If her performance is too openly presentational, it could convey the message that her primary purpose is to entertain them, and the self-respect of the character and her relationship to Touchstone might be compromised. If played directly to the audience, the actor will want to decide between doing so as actor or as character: for the reasons mentioned, the latter seems preferable.

This is another scene where Touchstone sees himself as the star, but this time in a somewhat different role: the courtly lover. One of his options for movement might therefore take the form of something like the Condescending Courtier Dance, largely consisting of a succession of sensitive–beautiful gentleman poses, connected by gliding movements in to Audrey for a touch before sliding away again. This is only one option for the actor, of course. Another might involve keeping very close to Audrey throughout, perpetually handling her. However it is performed, he has two audiences in the scene, one on and the other off stage.

5–6   The locale is Touchstone's Arden: somewhere in the neighbourhood of Audrey's goats, a practical (and probably smelly) place of real farm work. Most importantly, it is a locale where Touchstone thinks he doesn't fit (though for the purposes of comic contrast, he does), but which he enjoys being superior to.

6   It has been suggested that 'Goths' was pronounced 'goats' (see Hattaway, 2000, p. 147), though to do so might confuse the meaning of the sentence, at least for those who know about Ovid.

7–8   It seems almost as if Jaques has trundled off from his unfortunate encounter with Orlando to find a more receptive object for observation and interference. He reaffirms his status as a nosey, satirical gentleman priding himself on his superiority to mere clowns (and just about everyone else). He loves to give advice, which Touchstone responds to rather better than Orlando did.

7–65 There is the option of having Touchstone perceive Jaques's presence and play the scene with that awareness. The argument against this choice is that it could create too many points of focus in the stage action, since Touchstone would still have to play to Audrey and to the theatrical audience.

42–57 This whole speech could be addressed to an uncomprehending Audrey, but it can become more interesting if it is played to the audience as well, as it surely would have been on the Elizabethan stage. Some might want to compromise by playing it as a soliloquy, but, given the character, it would still have to be performed with full awareness of the audience's presence. The speech is somewhat different from Touchstone's usual efforts. He is not arguing with somebody, trying to show off his cleverness, but as close to thinking aloud as we could expect of him, though of course he can't refrain from making jokes. None the less, this is as serious as we have seen him. He seems to be really a little afraid of marrying Audrey, and indirectly tells us that his feeling for her is serious – though of course Touchstone's seriousness is hardly the same as, say, Orlando's. Who else would argue that cuckoldry is made honourable by marriage – except, in an oblique and ironic way, Rosalind (IV.i.159–67)?

67–8 The reference is to their previous meeting, described by Jaques in II.vii.12–42, in which Touchstone paraded his wit and wisdom to an apparently appreciative Jaques.

66–9 Touchstone the clown is the only one in the play to call attention to Jaques's name meaning a privy. Perhaps this is the recognition of a fellow clown, though also simply because it is his kind of humour. Their exchange of courtesies provides an opportunity for a bit of comic business about who should put on or take off his hat in the presence of the man of the church. (It is possible – though probably less rich in comic possibility – that 'pray be covered' is addressed to Audrey.)

66–88   Jaques's entrance will alter Touchstone's behaviour, for he is no longer performing for Audrey, but for a new, higher-status spectator. From being vain courtier he changes to fellow sophisticate, which might well involve several varieties of bowing and/or hat-doffing to Jaques. His first speech includes seven distinct greetings to a fellow courtier, each one a separate attempt to say the right thing. The speeches following these may be accompanied by more wrigglings and writhings as he plays apologetic mock modesty about being caught in the act of getting married to his 'toy in hand'. Lines 81–5 can be played either to the audience or confidentially to Jaques. If the latter, more insinuating contortions might again be appropriate as he speaks *sotto voce* to a fellow man of the world.

90–6   The brief song lyric at the end of the scene was set in the Folio as prose, and may have been spoken rather than sung. However, it provides an opportunity for Touchstone to show off again with much ironic bowing and a full song-and-dance exit – probably very badly sung.

97–8   This is a classic ending for comic scenes: after a sort of climax, the stoical, phlegmatic comic butt is left flat, but has the last, anti-climactic word.

Act III, scene iv (55 lines; approx. 3 minutes)

A 'holding scene', delaying further development of the Rosalind–Orlando interaction and introducing us to another complication in the Silvius–Phebe subplot. The theme of love continues to be developed, though this time it is its disappointed underside that is shown, with Rosalind petulant and Celia sarcastic. The sequence keeps alive the play's continuing current of irony. As so often in this play, the theme is handled not by poetic outpourings but by comic suffering and satirical references to literature and folk humour.

1–4   They are waiting in the neighbourhood of Rosalind's cottage, the place she was taking Orlando to at the end of their last scene together (III.ii.418). Rosalind again opens a scene with sadness, a constantly recurring pattern (see I.ii, I.iii, II.iv). This time, however, she displays a petulant self-pity we haven't seen before.

2–42   Celia's ironic remark in lines 2–3 is a satirical echo of Rosalind's own self-reminder at II.iv.3–7. Celia continues her teasing, repeating the same conventional notion Touchstone has just voiced (compare ll. 27–8 with III.iii.17–18), even using language of a kind the clown might have used. Celia's tone has become markedly different. Her sarcastic condemnations of love and of Orlando in particular seem more than just good-natured teasing, suggesting that her feelings for her friend have been tested – perhaps even torn – by Rosalind's love for Orlando. Several actors have mentioned the change in the relationship between the two, as Celia loses her friend (see, for example, Rutter, 1988, pp. 114–17).

31–4   A surprisingly casual reference to what might have been expected to be an important reunion. Of course, the plot requires that she not reveal herself. At the same time, there is another reminder that the lover has superseded the father, as has been suggested earlier (I.iii.10–11). An additional motivation for her not revealing herself to her father is Rosalind's increasing love of her game of deception, underpinned by her complete confidence that everything will come right in the end.

43–55   The change to verse is preparation for the high-flown language of Silvius and Phebe, which is to follow. After the introduction of love in Act I, scene ii, the use of verse in the love action (as opposed to the serious scenes with the two dukes) almost always provides a means of mocking the self-consciousness of that love. This contrast of form and content is exemplified by the difference between Orlando's love poems and his prose expressions of love as part of a dialogue. We are led to think that, at least in comedy and in the context of love, the nearer the language is to prose the more real is the emotion. If the dramatic situation does not contain real suffering, as is generally the case in comedy as opposed to tragedy, the dignity and elevation which verse gives to feeling runs the risk of making it seem like parody. Thus the verse in which Rosalind and Orlando speak of love, in Act I, scene ii, for example, tends to be restrained and unelaborated, whereas the extravagant verse of Orlando in Act III, scene i, is clearly parodic, as is the language between Silvius and Phebe.

53   Her love needs a bit of feeding just now, though the mention of Phebe's disdain might be a painful reminder that perhaps she too is being rejected.

55   The line points explicitly to the satirical metatheatre which is to come. At the same time, it might suggest some actual intention on Rosalind's part to become actively involved in the Silvius–Phebe affair. Since she really knows nothing about them, perhaps it is because she wants to work off her present frustration with Orlando by perversely getting involved in other people's romantic life and warning them how unreliable lovers can be. Perhaps the likeliest explanation is the simplest: she just can't resist an opportunity to play make-believe!

Act III, scene v (139 lines; approx. 7 minutes)

The scene sets in motion the play's third love affair. Introduced as a piece of theatre, it is like a neatly structured one-act play, with Phebe as the central character. The action is clear, compact and ends with a note of suspense. The locale change is technically interesting, since the action moves to another place (almost filmically) with virtually no passage of time.

The scene presents the sharpest critique of infatuation so far. At the start, it seems for a moment as if it might really going to be in the tone of the pastoral romance, but it quickly becomes realistic, satirical, even farcical. The highfalutin love-making of the conventional pastoral form is turned into wonderfully silly comedy by being acted out by very simple, ordinary people. The language, while it is verse, is almost realistic, with more unexpected figures and references to ordinary life than was customary in the euphuistic style of the contemporary pastoral.

The action has a pronounced metatheatrical quality, enhanced by the seeming artificiality of the lines and the theatrical stereotypicality of the lovers. Certainly, both Silvius and Phebe seem acutely aware of their roles as romantic lovers in a performance, so the scene has the quality of self-conscious play-acting by amateurs. What makes it more than mere satire is the comic confusion felt by these characters at the situation they find themselves in: such confusion is not only a part of being love-smitten, but also a definitive characteristic of farce.

1–7 Silvius's unrequited love is an echo of Orlando's, and illuminates the latter's character by showing us how silly he would be without his other traits to give him some weight and authority. Because Silvius's slavish devotion lacks such rounding and redeeming traits, it is a real challenge for the actor to find a way of playing the role without being boring or vapidly farcical. The solution probably lies in making the feeling real to the audience, so that his monomaniacal devotion is not only farcical but touching as well, especially when he seizes the few opportunities to revel in it, as in lines 28–31 and 99–104.

8–27 The comic literal-mindedness of this speech is the first clear indication that the scene is by no means out of a real pastoral romance, nor even a simple parody of the genre. The speech is, first, a satiric criticism, spoken by a supposedly romantic figure, of the romantic convention that the disdained lover is wounded to the death. What takes it beyond simple satire, however, is the lunatic literal-mindedness of the speaker, who seems more concerned with doggedly proving a point than anything else. This is a speech whose humourless pedantry would frighten away any but the most totally besotted lover.

8–139 What makes Phebe so effective a character is the impulsive energy she brings to everything she does: her strong rejection of Silvius's pathetic plea; her sudden passion for 'Ganymede' and her determination to do something about it, even if it means unscrupulously manipulating poor Silvius. Absolutely determined to get what she wants – all the while tending to get bogged down by her own literal-mindedness – she becomes a charming comic eccentric.

34   Rosalind's (and the actor's) playing of 'Ganymede' becomes here even more metatheatrical, involving yet another role: actor > Rosalind > 'Ganymede' straight > 'Ganymede' as Phebe's scornful love-object. This new role, however, is infused with emotion of a new kind, somewhat negative and exaggerated for the sake of effect.

34–66   The usual understanding of the motivation of this sequence is that 'Ganymede', to dissuade Phebe from her infatuation with himself, tells her she is ill-looking, while the audience can see that she is in fact a pretty young country girl. However, nothing but convention requires that Phebe be nice-looking. The director and actor might choose to cast the role as a rather rough shepherd girl, no more attractive than the 'foul' Audrey. (This might have been easier on the Elizabethan stage, where the part was played by a boy.) Both her own self-love and Silvius's romantic self-delusion would easily have overcome such a handicap. If this option is chosen, clearly the playing of 'Ganymede's' insults would have to be handled with more delicacy of feeling, though no change of intent.

34–80   Her further development of the new role reveals another aspect of Rosalind herself. The decision to involve herself in the Silvius–Phebe relationship is an extension of two earlier traits we have seen: the lover's desire to talk about/watch love in action (l. 53) and her critical attitude towards the folly of love, which we have seen from the start and most recently in the scene with Orlando. Her criticism is expressed with a new sharpness, however, possibly a result of her momentary disappointment in Orlando. Her treatment of Phebe is certainly far less tolerant than her handling of Orlando, who suffers from a comparable obsession. This harshness on 'Ganymede's' part is as much out of tune with the expected smoothness and gentleness of the pastoral as is Phebe's almost farcical literal-mindedness, both by different means emphasizing yet again that conventional pastoral love is a clumsy self-deception. There may be in all of this criticism of self-deception an implied criticism of comparable sentimentality in the audience.

69–70 This marks the beginning of the major complication in the Silvius–Phebe subplot, built upon another mistaken-gender game. The fun of it is apparent: girl mistakes girl-in-disguise for boy, while, in the other plot, boy, also mistaking girl-in-disguise for boy, has 'him' pretend to be boy-in-disguise. Such games were popular in comedies of the period (see the excerpt from Lyly's *Gallathea*, pp. 17–19 above), and were to some extent the consequence of female roles being acted by boy players. Making girl-in-disguise actually boy-in-disguise-as-girl-in-disguise added an additional piquant dimension to the whole metatheatrical business.

82–139 In this last, long virtual monologue, in which Phebe details, denies and rationalizes her infatuation with 'Ganymede', the language of pastoral love is turned into pure comic character speech, full of the hesitations, self-deceptions, contradictions and turnings of thought that characterize internal speech. Almost a variation on the sort of things Touchstone does (see its rhetorical likeness to iii.ii.13–21), it is a brilliant comic solo.

ACT IV

Act IV, scene i (208 lines; approx. 11 minutes)

One of the two longest and most delightful scenes of the play; the same locale as in Act III, scene ii. This is Rosalind's home ground more than it is Orlando's.

The greater part of the scene deals with the play's main theme of love in a way that is exuberant, ironic and realistic. Orlando's sentimental love for Rosalind is now put to the test – a test which he feels but doesn't quite yet understand. At the same time, a strong undercurrent of real feeling accompanies Rosalind's satirical mockery of love's foolishness. The result is a particularly effective summing up, in one scene, of the play's treatment of this theme.

The predominant metatheatre of the play is acted out here in a most elegant way. Rosalind's masquerade – including the double masquerade of the boy actor playing the role – displays how the theatrical permeates human life and behaviour, especially in love. While we may choose to 'believe' in the scene and in Rosalind's pretended role, sometimes almost as much as Orlando does, we are aware throughout that this is a double performance of two actions: a piece of imagined 'life' in that most theatrical of places, the Forest of Arden, and a very theatrical presentation on the stage.

The prose of this scene offers some of the best examples of the varied and lively language of *As You Like It*. Each character (even Celia, in only one or two short speeches) is given her/his own speech dynamic, tempo and rhythm. Jaques briefly shows us again his rhetorical presentation of the ego with yet another formal catalogue of human types to which he himself doesn't belong (ll. 10–15). Orlando's language displays his informal courtesy and fundamental good nature: it is simple, direct and fluently responsive. Rosalind's language is of course the most brilliant of the scene. Taking the initiative from the beginning, she carries the scene forward with remarkable momentum, without ever – except perhaps for the brief, rather acidic exchange with Jaques – losing her characteristic lightness of touch. Her language is full of figures drawn from life – she talks a lot about male and female social behaviour – and never loses the feeling of talking directly to another person. Above all, her language has remarkable pace and rhythm, though without ever seeming to be a hurried gabble: it is, in short, a positive gift to an actor.

Opening stage direction   Rosalind enters eagerly, with Celia following her, looking expectantly for Orlando, but is accosted by the unwelcome Jaques, who seems almost to have been lying in wait. He is again busy trying to increase his stock of 'interesting people', though he seems particularly eager to impress 'Ganymede'. In an interesting structural parallel, Jaques is again used, as in III.ii.248–89, to introduce a major scene between 'Ganymede' and Orlando. In both cases, he puts them into a sour temper, perhaps to make the lifting of spirits that follows more of a contrast.

1–36 The first sequence is a sort of delaying action. Hoping for Orlando, Rosalind is frustrated and annoyed by Jaques's appearance. Despite his ingratiating greeting, she responds with the same unfriendly mood and rhythm seen in Orlando's reactions (III.ii.249–89 – particularly ll. 278–85). Some have seen Jaques's approach to 'Ganymede' as an attempt at homosexual seduction – even 'darkly suggestive of rape' (Reynolds, 1988, p. 107) – and in some productions he has persistently tried to embrace her. Her rejection may be less sexual, however, than simply an expression of contempt for his self-absorbed affectations. She certainly tries more than once to get rid of him.

Entirely apart from the possibility of homosexuality, the character of Jaques moves closer to becoming a rather disagreeable eccentric, however clever a talker he may be. He is entirely self-absorbed. Whether he continues to amuse and engage an audience will depend very much on the acting: not just his own, but also how the actors of Orlando and Rosalind behave towards him. Rosalind in particular is normative in the play: her attitude towards other characters is likely to determine that of the audience. If she is only amused by him, they are likely to be as well, but if she shows genuine annoyance (as the lines suggest), then Jaques's character will probably seem less funny and less sympathetic.

15–16 This self-conscious assertion amounts to a statement that he is a performer who has invented his own role, or 'persona'.

24–36 Orlando comes happily in, momentarily distracting 'Ganymede'. S/he sees him, but quickly recovers and ignores him. Meanwhile, Jaques finally gives up and starts to leave, using either Orlando's entering line or 'Ganymede's' preceding line (both of which, while in prose, could scan as blank verse) as an excuse. More to keep Orlando waiting than to insult Jaques further, 'Ganymede' almost follows him off with a last, lengthy bit of mockery, then turns and 'accidentally' sees Orlando.

28 Orlando enters determined to treat 'Ganymede' as 'Rosalind': he has accepted the game as emotionally important for himself and seems ready to engage more deeply with this substitute 'Rosalind', eventually perhaps to the point of close physical contact, although different productions take different approaches to this. A decision about the degree of physical intimacy between them is very important in playing the scene. Orlando's tone as he enters is not really that of the lover addressing his beloved, but that of a young man talking playfully and intimately to a friend. It is this affectionate familiarity that sets the tone of the scene, allowing it to become, as it develops, simultaneously a pretended love scene and a happy exchange between two affectionate friends joining in a wonderful game together. Such a relationship of friends allows Rosalind's bravura performance the scope for the kind of gaiety and warmth we find in it, with the underlying seriousness kept beneath the surface. The famous German production by Peter Stein (described below, pp. 131–6) included a brilliant notion about the interplay between Orlando and 'Rosalind': it was played like a children's game, childishly flirtatious but utterly innocent. To use this approach may require a style of acting in the rest of the play that may not be desirable for actors without experience in Brechtian acting, but it can none the less be a stimulating idea for the actors of this scene.

Whatever the approach taken, it is crucial that both Rosalind and Orlando, in their individual ways, become caught up in the game and are expressing strong feeling for a person who is 'there' and not there. Both engage in make-believe with real emotions, which is exactly what acting is. The most grown-up love either of them can actually act out is in the subtext. In the end the sequence has to remain – sadly for Orlando – a scene of two young friends playing together rather than of two lovers fully and frankly engaging with each other. All the same, they skirt dangerously close to open sexuality. Obviously, Rosalind, pretending to be 'Rosalind', can respond to him explicitly as a man, but Orlando's sexual feelings are more ambiguous, for reasons told later: 'Ganymede', he tells his brother, 'is fair, / Of female favour, and bestows himself / Like a ripe sister' (IV.iii.86–7).

28–88 That 'Ganymede' is both Rosalind and 'Rosalind' is strongly underlined: in the course of the scene, one or the other of them refers to, or addresses, 'Ganymede' as 'Rosalind' eleven times (ll. 28, 40, 48,

62, 84, 107, 109, 128, 129, 168, 177), and the supposedly absent real Rosalind is referred to six times (ll. 60, 63, 68, 104, 149, 188). This remarkable pattern of repetition keeps the see-saw of the Rosalind identity shifting throughout the entire exchange, reflecting how the two lovers perpetually oscillate between realities just as the actor does between roles.

31   An echo of Orlando's earlier 'Monsieur Melancholy' (III.ii.288–9).

36   Finally turning away from the departing Jaques, s/he pretends to see Orlando for the first time and greets him with sarcastic surprise. The tartness s/he has shown to Jaques is carried over, but is now friendly.

36–106   This sequence illustrates a major point made throughout the play: lovers like talking about love. Such talk is an acting out of love each to the other. But also, and more importantly perhaps, love itself is shown to consist of the mutually pleasurable activity of talking to each other *about* love. Young love is enormously self-referential and self-conscious. In this way, the play presents a variation of the life-truth that love is largely a creation of the imagination (assisted by reading, music, etc.). Consequently, as with Orlando and Rosalind (and in a different way, Silvius and Phebe), the pleasure of lovers consists of spending much time simply talking to each other about being in love and 'what it means to *me*'.

36–190   In the seduction which follows, 'Ganymede' entirely sets the tempo and the choreography of their interaction. Orlando's conciliatory speeches and moves are inevitably countered by mock derision and rejections, as s/he continues, in the words of the famous boxing philosopher Mohammad Ali, to 'float like a butterfly and sting like a bee'. Though this is the emotional pattern of the scene, the movement may take different forms in different phases of the action. The first part, lines 36–62, is primarily a series of quick sparring blows by 'Ganymede', probably embarking on brief movements away from him, then returning to score a quick point. The primary feeling of the movement is of teasing him, drawing him closer. Lines

65–8 are a challenge. How s/he presents it could take different physical forms. One could involve moving away, making him follow, in increasing flights, culminating in the long set-piece of lines 89–103, which s/he might play breezily to the air (and the audience). Alternatively, s/he might approach him closely at line 66 and deal with him at close quarters more and more intimately, leading him on until the coy rejection of line 87, at which s/he turns away, only to move closer again for her ironic disquisition of lines 89–103. Being so close, s/he can readily switch to being soft and affectionate at line 106. The two will then be close to each other, perhaps even kneeling, ready for the wedding ceremony. After the marriage, the sequence about marital fidelity can be played in continued physical closeness. John Bowe, the Orlando of Terry Hands's 1980 production, has described how this part of the scene was played (see *Players of Shakespeare 1*, 1985, p. 74), which provides a useful example of one way the business can be handled. In that production, the whole exchange between 'Ganymede' and Orlando was presented as a frankly sexual one, and after the wedding 'Rosalind encourages pretend bed-games' as she describes how a wife might behave. Then, 'as Orlando makes to go, she rises and, pretending that she is naked, drops Celia's shawl, which they have been using as a bedspread. Orlando is so involved in the game, he almost imagines he sees his lover's body. This is too much, the games must cease and he must leave' (ibid., p. 74). Obviously, the decision about how physical Orlando's expressions of feeling for 'Rosalind' can become will be a major consideration in the alternative chosen.

40–5 A deliberate echo of 'Ganymede's' earlier mention of a lover's sighs and groans recording every hour as regularly as a clock (III.ii.297–9).

40–62 As any actor's pretence requires the assistance of the spectator, Rosalind's performance is helped by Orlando's eagerness to cast her in the role of his 'Rosalind'. In the interplay with his imaginary beloved, he is necessarily a kind of role-player himself and becomes 'Orlando', the imaginary 'Rosalind's' lover and bridegroom, a 'character' he more and more easily becomes as the scene progresses. In the course of the performance, his co-actor instructs his 'character' about the reality of love, however, thus teaching Orlando the role-player how to be a better, more mature lover.

63-4   Celia has been following their exchange closely from the start, no doubt with mixed feelings. Here, Rosalind's rather insistent 'I am your Rosalind' provokes her, in her role as ironic spectator, to put in a neat little joke intimating more than it says openly: its rather tart implication is that the 'Rosalind' of Orlando's imagination is more beautiful – that is, more worthy of love – than you, the real Rosalind. This interruption adds a little edge to the game Rosalind is playing and serves the purpose of bringing Celia back into the scene. She will have to play an important role in their performance in a few moments.

   Perhaps a bit taken aback by Celia's remark, Rosalind takes a deep breath and plunges into her brilliant end-game.

89-106   A familiar device in their dialogues: a long speech from 'Ganymede' about the realities of love and of women, provoking an impulsive declaration of love from Orlando, which is immediately exploited: see III.ii.395–415.

106   Some directors have chosen to introduce a literal piece of business here: 'Ganymede' follows the movement of an imaginary fly around Orlando's head and finally swats it on his stomach.

117-33   Though obviously irregular, this would none the less have constituted to Elizabethans a legal and indissoluble marriage. The player of Celia might decide to perform a satirical version of Sir Oliver Martext, though this could prove distracting.

131-4   A very short honeymoon. 'Ganymede' slips quickly back to earth, introducing him to the realities of married life.

138-67   Another jocular portrait of the female sex (compare III.ii.397–405), pretty much a conventional male view, but presented with playful irony. The theme of gender figures importantly in the scene, not only in Rosalind's commentaries but also in her modelling of gender behaviour. In her freedom and playfulness, she herself continues to exemplify a normative version of femininity which dominates the play. While she may be regarded as 'liberated', it is significant that it is primarily her male disguise which liberates her, allowing her a freedom she does not conspicuously show before taking it on, or when she takes it off at the end of the play. In scenes like this she is modelling not so much an absolute equality of genders as a comic ideal of free womanhood, an exposition of the difference between equals in a fictional world. The fact of the role being originally written for and played by a young male actor must always be taken into account.

168–90   There is surely a pause as Orlando is suddenly struck by the realization that, though his feelings have been strong and real, it has all been make-believe. Confused, even distraught, he cannot go on. He must leave. The pang he experiences will stay with him, we may imagine, and is still present when we next see him: 'I can live no longer by thinking,' he says (V.ii.50). Though 'Ganymede', after the pause, tries to recapture the playfulness, Orlando's responses become perfunctory and disconsolate.

191–208   There is a pause, as Rosalind watches him go. When he is finally out of sight, Celia bursts into laughter, perhaps with a touch of bitterness in it. Is she admiring Rosalind's performance or reprimanding her? Perhaps both. The bawdy joke about her 'nest' (l. 194) would, to an Elizabethan audience, have referred to what the boy player's doublet and hose were concealing. Beyond that, the remark can have two kinds of meaning, one admiring, the other critical.

195–207   This is the climax of Rosalind's expression of her love, and is deliberately hyperbolical. As ever, she is at once ecstatic in her love and aware of the absurdity of its extremity. In the last few moments of the scene, we see how all this play and tutelage has only strengthened the joyous love which is the spine of the character. Her very last line is entirely characteristic: completely in love and at the same time whimsically acknowledging the absurdity of her feeling of helplessness.

199–200   Perhaps provoked by Rosalind's entire self-absorption, Celia is accusing her friend of fickleness – presumably to herself, but Rosalind is too far gone even to register her wounded friend's complaint.

205–8   Celia sounds a sad note at the end. Her friend has 'married' and has just now called her not 'Celia' but 'Aliena'. This last speech has a touch of real loneliness, perhaps encouraging the audience to think she might be very ready now to find a love of her own.

Act IV, scene ii (19 lines; approx. 1 minute)

A break to fill the time until two o'clock, when Orlando has promised to return, the scene is an interlude in the fictive action of the play. It is now about three-quarters of the way through the performance (2069 lines out of 2722). There hasn't been a song since Act II, scene vii (if we exclude Touchstone's half-song at the end of III.iii.), more than half the play ago. Still the Forest of Arden, this time a slightly wilder part of the courtly–sylvan forest of Duke Senior and his lords; Jaques has returned to the company in which he is most comfortable.

   The scene is metatheatrical: a group of actors singing a song on the stage will certainly remind the audience that they are watching a theatrical performance. It is yet another of the frequently recurring presentational elements in the play. We are reminded that *As You Like It* has more songs than any other Shakespeare play.

Opening stage direction   In startling contrast to the ending of the preceding scene, the whole group come on loudly, having just completed the hunt, flushed with excitement and perhaps a little drunk as well. The carcass of a deer may be used (some productions have done this), which lends the scene a different kind of realism from what has been seen before. Some directors, such as Peter Stein, have seen it as a kind of ritualized nightmare (see Patterson, 1981, pp. 144–6).

1   In an oblique way, the song's lyrics keep the subject of love and marriage in the spectators' minds. They might sense a connection with the preceding scene, in which Rosalind has hunted and caught Orlando, who has, after all, called her the 'huntress' who his 'full life doth sway' (III.ii.4).

1–9   Jaques seems to have forgotten his tearful sympathy for hunted deer (II.i.25–63). Here he is the ringleader of the group, the one who thinks of things to do, in this case rather a pretentious idea, with a touch of the grotesque about it. His suggestion is taken up immediately. Antlers are produced – perhaps taken from a carcass brought on stage – and bound onto the head of one of the hunters, who is hoisted onto the shoulders of others, then carried around as the song is sung loudly. There may be little difficulties in getting all this done. There is the choice of making a routine of this kind skilful and cleanly executed and thus more picturesque and 'romantic', or messy and crudely carried out and thus darker and more primitive. Depending on the concept used, the sequence might even be performed as a sort of dark and cacophonous forest fantasy (implying some of the confusion in Orlando's mind, or preparing for the dream-like events of Oliver's narrative in the next scene).

14–19   Yet another mention of cuckoldry, reinforcing the link with Rosalind's capture of Orlando, in particular her saucy account of the fate of the snail (IV.i.57–60) and her implications of the inevitability of infidelity (IV.i.159–62). We are reminded as well of Touchstone's worldly wisdom on the subject (III.iii.42–57).

Act IV, scene iii (182 lines; approx. 9 minutes)

A little more than two hours after the end of Act IV, scene i; Rosalind's love affair has progressed about as far as it can go short of actual resolution, and other matters have to be attended to. In terms of dramatic action, this scene is a double one, moving two of the plots forward to the point where they demand some kind of fairly quick resolution. The play has been going on for some 106 minutes (2088 lines), and the audience will be looking forward to an ending.

1–2   Rosalind starts yet another scene in a state of agitation, which again seems to provide some of the energy for what she does in the action following.

1–74   The language of this first part of the scene is a clever mixture of prose and verse. Between Rosalind and Celia, the usual wry prose, but Silvius brings in his own simple kind of romantic verse, which is quickly perverted by 'Ganymede' into a tougher and sharper verse language – dynamically very close to prose. A shift to actual prose occurs in the sharp comments accompanying the mock-lofty verse of Phebe's letter. Prose continues until Oliver's entrance, where quite another kind of action and language takes over.

3–5   Celia's perception of Orlando is acute: he has shown the purity of his love, and his state of mind as he last left was certainly 'troubled'. Sharpest of all, however, is her likening him to the boy Cupid and her suggestion that it is all simply too much for him. Is 'sleep' a subtle preparation for the dream-like action of Oliver's ensuing narrative? Certainly encountering Oliver as he does must have seemed unreal to Orlando.

6–39   A little game of derogatory comments on Phebe is played here, started unwittingly by Silvius's description of how she looked as she wrote the letter. 'Ganymede' launches into an extended series of insulting descriptions, continuing and roughening his earlier comments to Phebe herself. Though they are clearly intended to try to put Silvius off her, and show his own lack of interest in her, they might none the less be – depending on the casting of Phebe – more or less accurate (see the commentary on III.v.34–66).

13–74   The playing of 'Ganymede 2' (that is, the young man involved with Phebe) is here developed more fully. It is very noticeable how different a 'character' this is from the 'Ganymede 1' who has been playing with Orlando. Rosalind's love of play-acting is, after her love for Orlando, her strongest motivation throughout the play. The roles she chooses to adopt and how she plays them tell the audience much about her character. The less sympathetic traits performed here must also be taken into account in developing a full under-standing of the Rosalind character.

44–63 A parody of the sort of poems the characters in *Rosalynde* write to each other. Compare the sonnet from Lodge's Phoebe to the disdainful Rosader (Orlando) (Bullough, 1963, pp. 240–1).

50–1 As Silvius predicted, Phebe's views have changed now that she is herself in love. Her notion of the power of eyes has certainly changed: compare these lines with III.v.10–27.

75–182 The surprise of Oliver's appearance is compounded by the complete transformation of the character. How can we account for such a change, aside from the pure convention of the romance? Especially in a modern performance, where both actors and audi-ences might worry more about credibility than in the Elizabethan theatre, the problem needs to be thought about, particularly by the actor of the role. Two ideas suggest themselves. First, there is the possibility that in his last meeting with Duke Frederick, in Act III, scene i, Oliver is so shocked that he begins to question his past conduct and attitudes. It is conceivable that the actor might so play the ending of that scene as to suggest something of this shock (see the commentary on III.i.18). A second and probably more useful suggestion might have to do with how the actor plays Oliver's narration about Orlando's saving him from the lion. The actor may suggest that this sharply traumatic event was experienced by Oliver as a violent waking from a nightmare, which worked as a kind of shock therapy to bring about a profound change of heart. The most important means of persuading us to accept the transformation is the character's (and actor's) own deeply felt wonder at what has happened to him. The audience's empathetic sharing in his wonder will make belief much easier. Also at work is our very willing suspension of disbelief in the theatre. The use of narrative also helps: this kind of abrupt character change is probably easier to accept when shown in a narrative long-shot than in a close-up of dramatic interaction.

77 The olive trees are of the same 'literary' species as the 'palm tree' of III.ii.173.

78–128   Celia's character is on the brink of – perhaps even beginning – a significant change. This can only be suggested non-verbally, since she has no more lines in the play after this scene. In view of her and Oliver's love, of which we learn in the next scene but one, the actor of Celia will usually want to suggest something of her response to him in this scene. The lines tell us little. It is she, not Roslaind, who immediately responds to Oliver – perhaps an immediate affinity? Is it remotely possible that her sisterly feelings for Rosalind make her susceptible to Orlando's brother, or that she feels some need to re-enact Rosalind's falling in love with Orlando? An important factor might well be the emptiness in her left by the loss of Rosalind as her only intimate: perhaps she is ready for love. It seems obvious that she is struck by him from the moment he enters and that her interest grows in the course of the scene. By the end, having been taken through his re-birth by his moving account, she will feel that in some way she knows him. What comes out of this meeting shows that she can be as impulsive as Rosalind, something the actor might want to give a little more emphasis to in earlier scenes. Recalling her practical empathy in Rosalind's first responses to Orlando in Act I, scene ii might also be helpful to the actor.

83–8   The descriptions don't match the ones given earlier in I.ii.262 and I.iii.111. Whatever their correctness, however, it is hardly likely that the roles can always be cast so that actors exactly match them. Directors can change the lines if they think audiences will be troubled or distracted by the discrepancies.

More importantly, the description of 'Ganymede' is the first we have had by another character, and reminds us that 'he' was so like Rosalind that he might have been mistaken for her brother (see V.iv.28–9). As previously suggested, the words 'like a ripe sister' may be a subtle giveaway of Orlando's sexually equivocal feelings about 'Ganymede'.

93–7   The bloody handkerchief is produced for the first time, but retained by Oliver, who might even put it back in his pocket. After her first shocked exclamation, Rosalind is silent for some time, fearful of its possible meaning. Her next line is an insistent enquiry about Orlando's safety.

98 A new kind of metatheatre is frankly introduced: storytelling. The actor playing Rosalind, who has been the dominant metatheatrical performer of the first part of the scene, now becomes a susceptible spectator (along with Celia) as another actor takes the stage to tell a story to both onstage and offstage audiences.

98–156 Having decided to include the lion episode from Lodge's original, Shakespeare obviously had to treat it by narrative means, with several advantages ensuing. Orlando's final act of physical heroism is better narrated than shown. And who better to tell the story than the brother who had tried to kill him and whom he now saves from death? Another important benefit of using narrative here is that it creates an opportunity at a very advantageous point in the plot to remind the audience that Rosalind's love is more than merely playful by showing her profound shock at Orlando's wounding. In making these choices, Shakespeare encountered seeming difficulties. First, the narrative might have been felt to be a disturbance of the stylistic flow of the play, coming at a point where the stage action has been moving briskly. Shakespeare's structural sense is again sure, however, for the scene provides a kind of rhythmic pause and change of mood which help to prepare the audience for the considerable change of treatment that occurs in the last act. Another difficulty to be met at this point was the necessity of bringing Oliver and Celia together without the means Lodge used in *Rosalynde*: an extended rescue by him and his brother of 'Ganimede' and 'Alinda' ('Aliena') from robbers, which provided a credible time-span for love to blossom between them. That he was aware of this motivational difficulty is apparent in the attention given to it in Act V, scene ii, but obviously it is not regarded as a very serious problem for a theatrical audience (as opposed to readers of fiction).

The more immediate problems of this passage have to do with how the actor should play it. In the course of the lengthy narration, Oliver works himself through his emotional journey. Though he uses the conventional devices of the storyteller, he is caught up in his story, not only because the events were so intense and thrilling, but also because he is re-enacting the transformation of his own life and personality from villainy and wretchedness (ll. 106–7) to reconciliation and re-birth. The first part of the story (ll. 98–132) amounts to a kind of nightmare vision for him, and he would probably tell it accordingly, seeing it again before his eyes as he does so. The second part of the narrative (ll. 139–56), though the events are not so stark, might still have, for him, a feeling of unreality, of a new life so unexpectedly delivered to him and a new closeness to his once-hated brother.

127   Oliver employs the traditional storyteller's trick of making the listener wait.

133–4   It is only here that 'Ganymede' and 'Aliena' suddenly realize Oliver's identity. Up to this point, they have been entirely occupied with Orlando's possible fate.

138   Again, the storyteller's creation of suspense.

156–82   The metatheatricality of the impersonation of 'Ganymede 1' changes significantly from the beginning of the Oliver scene. For the first time in Rosalind's playing of the 'character', there is danger of being found out and fear of its happening. This completely changes the motivation and feeling of the masquerade. Though she is still as intent as ever on preserving the deception, what has been a love game seems to have become something more serious – though it is not clear how or why. After all, it seems that she simply doesn't want her real identity revealed until she is ready. Beyond sheer wilfulness, two motives for this seem possible. First, she is too proud of her play-acting skills to want to be found out in such a humiliating way. Secondly, she wants the final revelation to Orlando to occur at a time and in a way that suits her purposes, which in the end appear to be both educational and matrimonial.

156   The timing of her swoon and the reason for it are sometimes debated. Its placement here could be the result of having heard of Orlando's faint a few lines earlier, combined with Oliver not giving her the napkin until this point. Actually touching it could be what provokes her faint, though of course she has been made susceptible by Oliver's harrowing story and by simple relief at learning, at last, that Orlando is alive.

157–60   As both Celia and Oliver bend over the prostrate youth, perhaps they are drawn together by their shared concern: another possible hint towards making believable the two falling in love. Some productions – for example, Peter Stein's and Lucy Bailey's (see below, pp. 135, 142) – have dealt with the problem head-on by having the two fall into each other's arms as they minister to the unconscious Rosalind. The question of when they fall in love – if that can be pinpointed or *needs* to be pinpointed – is, like the same question in Act I, scene ii, to be worked out between the actors in rehearsal.

166–7   In the original performances, it is very likely that this bit of actor's braggadocio would have been addressed directly to the audience – as it may be today.

179–80   Why does he call her 'Rosalind'? Some commentators have suggested this means he knows her real identity, though we must remember that he knows no other name for the 'shepherd youth'. (Besides, if he did know, he would probably tell Orlando and the final scenes of the play would be impossible.) The actor must be careful here not to seem to know too much: perhaps through some clearly masculine friendly gesture?

182   'Rosalind', moving as jauntily as s/he can manage, goes on ahead, leaving Celia and Oliver to walk together – perhaps seeing what has started between them.

ACT V

Act V, scene i (62 lines; approx. 3 minutes)

A brief scene of comic relief, with William, a true country bumpkin, introducing a new note. As would be expected, the scene is entirely in prose. With the exception of Touchstone's pretentious displays of mock learning, the language is simple and direct. In his three longer speeches, Touchstone's language plays with conventional forms from rhetoric, logic, and the law.

By dealing in a simple way with love and the foolishness it gives rise to, the scene nicely offsets both the more serious and the more satirical treatments we have previously seen. The contrast between plain country behaviour and the affectations of the court is again played with.

1–4 An audience might well think they already sound like a married couple.

3–4 Audrey's 'old gentleman' is a very useful addition to the characterization of Jaques, summing up his behaviour and appearance as perceived by an innocent.

6–9 Perhaps really worried or perhaps only to avoid further pestering, he brings up the possibility of a rival suitor. Audrey means 'no claim to me', though the modern director might choose to keep the line, changing 'in' to 'for'.

10–12 This is unmistakably directed to the audience. It is possible to address it to Audrey, but Touchstone's vain display seems less to her than to the world – his world, that is, which is the theatre audience.

13–59 Another star turn by Touchstone, following the same basic cross-examination pattern as III.ii.11–84, though of course with many differences. The 'accused' in the two cases are both countrymen, but very dissimilar characters. More specifically, Touchstone is much more aggressive towards William, for obvious reasons. The sequence is reminiscent of the meeting of two competing suitors leading up to a duel, and in this respect is a subtle foreshadowing of Touchstone's claim in V.iv.46–7 and his ensuing set-piece on the protocol of courtly duelling. There are various options as to how Touchstone might move during the sequence, one of which could be another of his 'dances'. It would no doubt have a number of clearly distinguished elements (a little like the Degrees of the Lie in V.iv.48–102), including such as the following:

1. The Approach (for example, l. 16): he moves towards his opponent in a manner both ingratiating and threatening.
2. The Confrontation (ll. 20, 22, 24, 27, and so on): he closes in on the opponent – sometimes coming closer than is comfortable – in order to impose his presence.
3. The Question (the spoken elements of ll. 20, 22, 24, 27, and so on), delivered either as a seemingly innocent enquiry (ll. 20, 22, 24, 35) or as a more threatening bit of interrogation (l. 37).

These elements constitute the preliminary, more intimate phase of the dance. Overlapping with this phase is the second stage (beginning with the responsive bits in ll. 16–17, 26–7, and getting fully under way at l. 29). In this second part, Touchstone may begin to take space around his opponent, using the stage more fully, but keeping the other as the centre of his circular movement, and incorporating such elements as these:

4. The Reactive Twirl (for example, ll. 26–7): reacting to what has just been said to him, he makes a happy twirl, which brings him back around to face his quarry.
5. The Cogitative Circle (ll. 29–35): the idea that seizes him takes him into a thoughtful circling either around or in front of his antagonist.
6. The Sombre Statement (ll. 39–43): after fixing his opponent with a dark look, Touchstone may approach him slowly, very portentously delivering an important truth; in some cases, the Sombre Statement may be extended into:
7. The Death Threat (ll. 45–57): the victim is subjected to a serious, extended explanation whilst being backed across the stage.

These of course are only the outer frameworks of dance movements: how the body is used in executing them is crucial to their effectiveness. As ever, the individual actor will wish to develop his own idiosyncratic gestures and movements. There are of course other options for the actor in playing this scene, but it seems central to the sequence that William is the immobile (probably unfazed) victim and Touchstone the ominous stalker.

15–17 Another hat routine, probably more elaborate than Jaques and Touchstone at III.iii.69. William has the opportunity of taking his hat off and putting it back on at least three times, twice from verbal instruction and at least once more in response to a look. The principle of the *lazzo*, if it is used, is that he simply feels unbearably uncomfortable in Touchstone's presence with his hat on and will therefore take it off again at any slight provocation. William is of course unfailingly polite throughout.

45 It seems that Touchstone has reached the point where his clownish lust for Audrey has grown to clownish love. Marriage is definitely on.

58 Even more clearly than in her earlier scene, Audrey proves herself a good-natured girl with a kind heart: compare her rejection of William with Phebe's very different treatment of Silvius in III.v.8–34.

59 If played with the utter imperturbability he has shown throughout the scene, this line might well leave the audience wondering whether William has actually understood a word Touchstone has said.

62 Touchstone virtually skips off, in a state of high elation after totally routing his rival. The very slight Touchstone–Audrey love plot has effectively been resolved; only the formality of a wedding remains. The play has therefore reached the point where the various sets of lovers must be brought together and their fates settled.

Act V, scene ii (125 lines; approx. 6 min)

The action returns to the first of the Forest sublocales, where Duke Senior has established his sylvan court: in effect, a move back towards civilization, which the action confirms. The scene is devoted to tying up any loose ends before the final resolution, while at the same time starting the transition into the formality of the final wedding scene.

For most of its length, the scene is in plain, practical prose, lending a simple down-to-earth quality to Oliver's description of his love, Rosalind's lively account of the stages of love and Orlando's simple declaration of his own state of mind, and then, finally, a credible straightforwardness to Rosalind's assertion of her qualifications as a magician and her plan to bring Orlando the happiness he so longs for (and finally deserves). With the entrance of Silvius and Phebe, the language moves briefly into verse, then into an entirely different, highly formal kind of prose for the rest of the scene.

1–16 Ironically, Orlando's questions are those of a responsible older brother, not a younger one, and show at the same time how very different his attitude towards love has become. The mere idea of love is no longer enough, it must be persevered in. He seems to accept his new status very quickly, for his granting of consent is the action of the squire towards a lesser person.

5–12 After joy at being re-born during his forest rescue and reconciliation with Orlando (IV.iii.135–7), Oliver now completes his transformation not only by loving his 'Aliena' but by renouncing his former status and becoming a shepherd (a foreshadowing of Duke Frederick's comparable conversion – see V.iv.153–63). His tone has become authoritative without his previous harshness, and his language is transformed into a very formal, balanced prose, preparing us for the recitations of the later part of the scene.

9–12 Making over his properties to his younger brother resolves the issue initiated in Act I, scene i, and foreshadows the comparable act on Duke Frederick's part (V.iv.162–4). The question remains, however, as to whether he still owns the house and revenue after Duke Frederick's confiscation. The problem is resolved at V.iv.163–4 and 167–8.

17–18   The words 'sister' and 'brother' are both ironic and whimsical. He greets her as his brother's 'Rosalind', she him as the betrothed
of her 'sister' 'Aliena' (see IV.iii.88). Even more noticeable in the scene
is that the name 'Ganymede' is no longer used, except by Phebe.

19–50   Appropriately, Orlando and 'Rosalind', though her
'Ganymede' disguise is maintained, seem on more intimate terms
since the mock wedding. She is now, quite casually and comfortably,
'Rosalind' (l. 16).

19–125   Rosalind here begins the final phase of the character's
development, a change not back into her original self, but into a
mature figure of authority in the lives of the other characters – an
authority she has already casually used in her dealings with
Orlando. This impression is strengthened by the fact that in this
scene she is the one who knows everything, while the others still
remain in ignorance. Her performance of the role of 'Ganymede'
becomes more serious and less ironically playful. When she speaks
to Orlando, it is as an equal, not as a lovesick young woman or a flip-
pant youth. She now has the maturity to manage the lives of others
with confidence.

28–40   'Ganymede' reverts to his earlier jaunty self in this little
performance piece. It has a similar tone and progressive structure to
what we hear from 'him' elsewhere (for example, III.ii.297–327 and
III.ii.395–412), and to that found in the standard comic set-pieces of
Jaques (II.vii.139–66) and Touchstone (V.iv.67–102). But Orlando
breaks the mood, returning to the business of weddings and to his
own sadness.

50   Meaning, 'No more playing'. This marks a conclusive shift in
the character and the play, a change which has been in the making
since IV.i.168. As one measure of the character change, we might ask
ourselves if we can imagine this Orlando writing and posting the
poems we have heard. At this point, he has finally acknowledged that
dreaming is no substitute for reality, while Rosalind has perhaps
learned that she has been hard on him, playing with his emotions so

freely. There is certainly a pause following the line, after which Rosalind efficiently moves to resolve everything.

51–74   The necessity for a real resolution of the Rosalind–Orlando plot has been established and 'Ganymede' promptly sets things in motion. It is, however, to be accomplished by means entirely different from any earlier action in the play (though not uncommon in comedies of the period). A character who has been the clever manipulator of everything so far now displays a new skill: magic. To Elizabethans, this would have been something very like witchcraft, though the magic is white, not black. By suggesting that events from now on will be determined by supernatural means, Shakespeare moves the play into fantasy, which alters the meaning of what will happen. The outcomes will be made a little less 'natural', a little more artificial and arbitrary. At the same time, the fact that these events are determined by a mere 'boy' helps to perpetuate a feeling of playfulness even in the midst of ceremonial seriousness. 'Ganymede's' explanation of how he will accomplish a resolution very much resembles (and might well be delivered in the manner of) the circumstantial *spiel* a magician conventionally uses to prepare his audience for the trick, including a description of his powers and a reassurance that the subject being summoned from another world (l. 65) will be exposed to no 'danger' and will appear 'before your very eyes', in the flesh ('human as she is').

60–1   A similar fictitious figure to the 'old religious uncle' of III.ii.336–7.

76–82   The movement into the ceremonial is only briefly interrupted by Phebe's complaint (in verse, after prose thus far in the scene). After 'Ganymede's' insensitive rejection, it is Phebe, ironically, who appeals to true romantic feeling with her command to Silvius to tell her beloved what love really is.

83–125   Silvius's heartfelt declaration – very different from his earlier effusions – is turned by the incantatory responses of the others into a liturgy of love, transforming the rest of the scene into ceremony, with only Rosalind's tart interpolations as relief. It is a preparation for the weddings to follow, when these formal declarations of love, devotion and frustration will become avowals of commitment. The sudden formality of this passage, in which the participants become ritual celebrants, creates a new kind of metatheatricality, a reminder that theatrical performance itself is historically based on ceremony and ritual. At the same time, it is striking how the ritual form of the responses gives dignity to what might otherwise have been more of the same pastoral sentimentality.

Act V, scene iii (45 lines; approx. 3 minutes)

This scene is in simple comic prose, with the obvious exception of the song's lyrics, which are in the manner of a traditional folk song, including its cheerful refrain. The scene is a little like a jig, for which it may have been a partial substitute (they were being discontinued by about this time), though Rosalind's Epilogue also performs a jig-like function. Primarily a musical prelude to the nuptials to come 'tomorrow', the scene is straightforwardly metatheatrical, almost entirely dominated by the pages' performance of the song (accompanied by suitably unsuitable business).

1 The echo of 'tomorrow' from the preceding scene strongly suggests that this scene should follow it without a pause. The song and Touchstone and Audrey's interaction are, after all, an immediate, farcical acting out of the sexuality underlying the preceding scene.

1–5 Audrey is as simple and unaffected as ever, while Touchstone seems to have settled down a bit and appears to really want to marry his country lass. His opening line seems intended to be taken as sincere, but the actor is free to choose otherwise: clownish lechery and irony may still flourish. In either case, it can be presumed that he and Audrey are engaged in some kind of physical business, and her reference to the pages' entrance might be accompanied by her awkwardly disentangling herself from Touchstone's gropings.

5   The pages are new characters, though they may have appeared as
extras in previous scenes at the Duke's encampment, and may also
serve a similar function in the wedding ceremony to come.

8–37   The invitation to 'sit' and to 'sit i'th' middle', followed by the
repetition of the song's refrain, seems to suggest some repeated physical business among the four of them, perhaps involving Touchstone
repeatedly cuddling (an embarrassed?) Audrey and the pages trying
at one time or another to join in, forcing Touchstone to push them
off: a fair tangle could ensue.

41–2   Meaning, perhaps, they didn't lose a beat while fooling
around with Audrey?

44–5   In the original performances this may have been a joke about
the changing voices of boy players.

Act V, scene iv (197 lines; approx. 10 minutes)

The play has reached the point where everything is to be settled, with
only the details of 'how' left to be disclosed: Rosalind's identity must
now be revealed, Silvius and Phebe's relationship repaired, and – if
total resolution is to be achieved – the conflict between the two
dukes somehow resolved. The much-announced weddings will be
romantic endings, not realistic beginnings. Love is now a serious
matter, involving the consequence of marriage, though we have
earlier heard that there is more to it than that. More important
perhaps is the different forms love can take, evidenced by the variety
of couples on display. Another major theme, the contrast of false
courtly and natural country life, is equivocally resolved by the
presentation of a now legitimized 'country court', where the ranks
and decorum of conventional courtly life are to be observed. The
related subject of true versus false authority is comfortably resolved
by Duke Frederick's conversion, and restitution of the usurped dukedom to his brother. These thematic resolutions seem rather superfi-
cial and too convenient, however. In comedies like this, the
convention calls for such a restoration of the status quo, which is

seemingly justified in the end on the assumption, common in Elizabethan times, that the established order of the world is essentially ordained by God and thus not to be questioned. Divine approval of the conventional pairings and restoration of property is suggested by Hymen in lines 107–9. For a modern audience, however, the very formulaic nature of the assertion of order may deprive it of weight and authority.

The treatment of gender differences also reaffirms the traditional and conventional, with the implied acceptance by Rosalind of her role as a woman subservient to her husband. It remains a subtext of this scene, however – which might slightly comfort a modern audience – that this affirmation of the status quo was made possible and arranged by the powers of a woman, albeit a most extraordinary one. Perhaps a further word on this theme will yet be spoken, in the Epilogue.

Metatheatricality is strong: ritual, song and dance predominate, reminding us of the ceremonial in life itself, especially on its festive occasions. The language of the scene, as we might expect given its different actions, is variable, adjusting to the shifts of action and style as the scene progresses.

Opening stage direction   The omission of the two older characters, Adam and Corin, may be because of the scene's focus on youth and happy beginnings, but is more likely to be because in the original performances it may have been required by the necessity for double casting.

1–4   An obvious device to prepare for 'Ganymede's' entrance and ratchet up the suspense one last, tiny notch, as well as allowing a few moments for Rosalind, Silvius and Phebe to make their entrance. The presiding presence of Duke Senior at the opening makes it clear the resolution will have authoritative approval.

1–34   This is the first of the scene's five distinct segments (six, counting the Epilogue), each of which is quite different in content, tone and language. This one is dominated by the last appearance of 'Ganymede', who comes briskly in, all business, and proceeds to address each person, like a sports teacher ensuring that every pupil knows exactly what to do. The effect is to demonstrate that the time of free choice – even for Phebe – has passed: what comes next is fixed and ordained by the rules. The action in this scene is no longer dramatic action in the usual sense; it has been taken out of the characters' hands and made into a prescribed formula arranged by the master of ceremonies acting for some higher authority.

5–25   The formulaic style of the preceding scene is continued with the very literal-minded repetition of demands and promises. Even more than before, these formalities foreshadow the questions and responses of the marriage ceremony. The question arises of why it is necessary to spell out all of these commitments with such particularity, especially since the only matter about which there can be any doubt is Phebe's acceptance of Silvius if she loses 'Ganymede'.

8–10   'Kingdoms' foreshadows the restitution of the Duke's dukedom and Orlando's becoming heir to it, and their return to the world where such hierarchies will again rule.

25   Celia, who has been present dressed as 'Aliena', Oliver's prospective 'shepherdess'-bride, now quietly goes out with 'Ganymede', perhaps with a sly smile at her puzzled bridegroom.

26–34   Duke Senior and Orlando are still wondering about this remarkable boy. If it weren't for the suspension of normal dramatic credibility, the Duke's failure to recognize his own daughter – though the 'shepherd boy' does look kind of familiar – might make a thoughtful spectator wonder how close they ever were. Recalling his own first impression of 'Ganymede', Orlando suggests another reason why he might have been so ready to imagine 'him' as his 'Rosalind'. Now, however, having given up hope of finding his Rosalind by normal means – though the man standing next to him is her father – he desperately needs to believe that the boy's powers, acquired in the hidden magician's circle of the forest, will secure her for him. All of this makes it more than clear that the play is now in a different world, however it may slightly resemble the previous one, and that the actors playing these two roles had best focus on playing the strangeness and wonder of the event rather than on the commonplace particulars of their own relationship.

35–42 This starts the second of the scene's six segments. Jaques's announcement deliberately shifts the mood from serious expectation to comic introduction, hailing back to II.vii.12–43 and his subsequent meetings with Touchstone, and bringing their relationship to a sort of culmination with his introduction to the Duke. At the same time, his mention of Touchstone's claim to be a courtier reminds us that we are back in the courtly world, or soon will be. Finally, there is the further suggestion that Jaques, in his role of master of entertainment to the Duke, is introducing the main performer for the wedding occasion.

38–106 Touchstone makes a big entrance to the exalted wedding venue, no doubt specially dressed for the occasion, with Audrey – in her own version of fine attire – as his obedient stooge (who may have 'costume-malfunction' problems at ll. 67–8). In this performance – one of the most important of his life, since his future employment may well depend on it – he is again the star, but performing to a very difficult audience. In the first place, he has no supposed inferior to play to, play down to and play off. Secondly, his main audience is the Duke, a very exalted figure.

His performance is likely to involve much physicality, perhaps an elaborate 'dance' dividing itself into several segments. There is a brief opening exchange of courtesies with the Duke (ll. 51–6), with much bowing and hat-play, followed by various writhing apologies for his presence in these 'copulative' circles and for the dowdy beloved by his side. When his routine gets properly under way, Touchstone, in the absence of the living foil he normally requires, has to create an imaginary opponent, introduced in line 47. (It is possible that he might use Jaques for this purpose, which could lead to comic interplay between them in the course of the routine.)

If the actor chooses to perform the sequence in such a way, the dance can be executed with this fictional antagonist placed in the centre, whom he then proceeds to 'send word to', approach, bow to, deliver a series of Retorts, Reproofs, Counterchecks and Lies to – all with appropriate gestures and grimaces. The dance becomes an extended enactment of the whole absurd ceremony of courtly duelling, spoken with great speed and skill, and culminating in the handshake and swearing of brotherhood in line 101. His reward is to receive from the Duke the kindest (and least accurate) compliment he has received in the whole play, which may well lead Touchstone to think his professional future is assured, whatever the fate of his marriage.

103–4 Is Jaques recommending Touchstone to succeed him as the Duke's jester?

106 stage direction She returns, no longer Rosalind, but an emblematic figure of the bride. Though she is normally thought to be returning to her original identity, no audience is likely to think this is the case. Her full personality has been released and gloriously acted out, so what she seems to become now is something much less. If we look for convincing motivation – which may be quite irrelevant in this kind of sequence – we can only think that she behaves here as the occasion requires her to behave, doing so out of real love, but without intending in her future life to turn into a merely obedient, well-behaved wife: she has earlier (IV.i.138–67) given us cause to doubt that. Therefore, while her transformation in this final ceremony seems magical (as, in one way or another, all the transformations of serious characters have been), we can still believe that the real changes in her character in the course of the play have been humanly true.

106–49 The actors in the final part of the scene – assuming that they do not want to be mere mannequins in an artificial masque – have to deal with the difficult task of finding a way of performing in such a formal, unreal ceremony without losing some feeling of their characters. The answer may lie in each performing her/his part in the ceremony in her/his own way – taking a 'Touchstone approach' as it were – thus providing a sense of the character within the masque figure, and perhaps conveying something of her or his attitude towards the ceremony: a situation not unlike a real-life wedding!

107–49   In the third segment of the scene, prepared for and introduced by the Duke's courteous conclusion of the comic introduction, the music constitutes a continuation but a change in the nature of the entertainment. After Hymen's song – or recitation – there follow speeches spoken in an almost trance-like state, as the characters are caught up in the unearthly atmosphere. An oddly provisional nature is given to events by the repeated use of 'if', which is, as well, a repeated, ironic echo of Touchstone's 'If is the only peacemaker'. It is likely that a director may choose to continue the 'still' music under the blurring and doubling of characters' focus and their dream-like confusion, accompanied by a drifting of the wedding couples into appropriate positions around Hymen. He loftily re-takes command of the occasion and proceeds to perform the marriage ceremony. The song is probably sung by everybody present and any accompanying movement might want to be limited and rather ceremonial, since this is a hymn and the real dance is yet to come.

115–16   The dream-like formality of expression could obscure Rosalind's acceptance here of a return to the traditional position of woman as subservient to father and husband, an acceptance repeated in lines 121–2. These lines seem to show the Rosalind/'Ganymede' character disappearing into the nuptial mist. The actor of the role retains the option, however, of performing them – and playing the character's silences in most of the rest of the scene (except of course the Epilogue) – in a way to suggest to Orlando (and the audience) that the Rosalind they have known is still here and has not forgotten her earlier description of what their marriage will be like (IV.i.138–67), even though she is willing to behave submissively for the moment.

134–5   For Touchstone and Audrey, a stormy but not unsuitable marriage, perhaps not so short-lived as Jaques predicts in lines 190–1.

146–9   Spoken as if just having waked, with a touching sincerity, and briefly effecting the two reunions not quite completed till now. The Duke's acceptance of Celia as a 'daughter' reminds the audience of her and Rosalind's 'sisterhood' and echoes her early remarks about sharing a father, particularly in I.ii.10–11. Phebe's acceptance of Silvius is made more credible by the fact that not only is she keeping her promise, but his faithfulness has finally 'combined' (bound) her 'fancy' (love) to him.

150–78   The scene's fourth segment begins with another abrupt shift of style. It is another visitation by an unknown figure, who, like Hymen, plays *deus ex machina*. This speech is almost exactly like the messenger speech with which a number of Greek tragedies end.

158–61   The conversion of Duke Frederick by 'an old religious man' introduces yet another mysterious elderly man (following 'Ganymede's' 'old religious uncle' at III.ii.335–6 and his 'magician' at V.ii.61 and V.iv.33), summoned up out of the murky forest depths to explain the inexplicable or perform the impossible.

162–74   The Duke's status and his lands are restored, as well as those of the Lords of his court and those of Oliver. The change is made official by the Duke himself, who adds to it the elevation of Orlando to become his heir, perhaps required by the fact that Oliver, having now got his properties back, will want to keep them, despite the gift mentioned in V.ii.10–12. All these practical arrangements underline that the return from Arden means a return to the rules and conditions of the real world: each will be restored to good fortune in accordance with his or her traditional and fixed social status. This will presumably include the return of Rosalind to the position she held before her exile and adventures in freedom. Her acceptance of this return to the 'normality' of subservient wifedom has been suggested in lines 115–16.

179–95   The fifth segment of the scene begins with Jaques characteristically stopping the music – perhaps a moment or two after it has begun, so as to maximize the impact of his interruption. His decision, the equivalent of going into a monastery, might be because his hopes for 'Ganymede's' love have been dashed (in which case, his reaction to Rosalind's reappearance as herself at lines 106 might want to be pointed out somehow). Another, more likely reason, however, is that he is continuing his perpetual interest in meeting and quizzing 'interesting people', as we have seen him doing with Touchstone, Orlando and 'Ganymede'. It is also a decision not to return to the world of the court, but to remain in Arden, where perhaps he feels safest and most comfortable. (See below, p. 158, for Jan Kott's comment on Jaques's motives at the end of the play.)

196–7   A wedding dance had been the traditional ending for comedy since Greek times. Its placement here – before the Epilogue – seems to have been Shakespeare's intention, thereby giving added importance to the Epilogue as the last thing the audience heard. Modern productions have handled it in different ways, depending on how they wanted to bring the performance to an end.

197   The scene is as final as a final scene can be, even if its resolutions are arbitrary or provisional. But the central subject of the main plot, the identity of Rosalind, apparently culminating in her wielding the power to resolve other people's lives, is then unsettled by her final appearance as a sexual emblem apparently acquiescing to a gender stereotype. Especially in view of this disappointment and despite the apparent finality of this scene, something remains unsaid, something for which the whole play has prepared us but which has not yet been openly spoken. While the last scene ends the dramatic action, it does not end the play's theatrical statement.

Epilogue (23 lines; approx. 1 minute)

Stage direction following lines 197   Behind the actor delivering the Epilogue the stage may still, in some productions, represent the Forest of Arden. As the actor speaks, however, s/he strips the stage of its illusion, as it were, revealing it to be what it always was (and the audience always really knew it was): simply a stage. As this happens, the audience is made aware of what, in fact, they have actually known, subliminally and happily, during the entire performance: they have been in two places at once!

For the first time in the performance, an actor is seen by the audience not in relation to other characters or performers, but frankly as her/himself. Only in this way can the creation of the complex theatrical identity called 'Rosalind' be completed. This last appearance of the Rosalind player epitomizes the essential metatheatricality which has permeated the play, especially since the end of the second act. In the course of the performance, there have been frequent instances of actors addressing the audience, sometimes as actors, sometimes as characters, sometimes as both. Now an actor appears alone, addressing the spectators as both character and performer – and pointedly calls attention to the fact of her/his double identity. In doing so, s/he shines a light back upon the whole play and performance, saying, 'Look. This is what we have been doing here.' This frank address to the audience is the culmination of the intimate and celebrative relationship the Rosalind player has built between her/himself and the spectators. The key element in that relationship has been play. Suitably, it is the sly playfulness of the Epilogue which best summarizes the audience's experience of the play, sending them home in the end to carry on playing – as they like it.

198–200   Among other things, the Epilogue specifically and pointedly plays with the question of the relative status of 'lady' and 'lord', who later become 'men' and 'women'.

208   'Conjure' refers not only to the skills demonstrated by 'Ganymede', but also to the actor's own magical skills of creating illusion at will.

213–14   'Play' obviously has a double meaning, compounded by the fact that the play's title, *As You Like It*, could be a colloquial synonym for love-making. More importantly, the line is a final affirmation of the principle of achieving gender equality through play, as Rosalind's 'Ganymede' performance has repeatedly demonstrated.

214–15 'If I were a woman' may create problems for the female actor of the role: some have suggested changing it to 'If I were among you'. But spectators may have less difficulty with the line than might be expected. First, it is quite simply a kind of joke and will be taken as one. Secondly, the actor can be understood to be saying 'If I were a woman as you would like a woman to be' (as in the ideal 'Rosalind'), while implying that a real woman will not be quite so obliging (as the Rosalind/'Ganymede' has repeatedly asserted).

With respect to gender, the Epilogue ends in ambiguity about the identity of the actor in the theatre. Is the person who speaks these words (and then disappears) a real woman or some kind of androgyne? Catherine Belsey speaks of Rosalind at this point as occupying 'a place which is not precisely masculine or feminine, where the notion of identity itself is disrupted' (Belsey, 1985, p. 187).

219–20 Having made a 'kind' (but equivocal) offer of a suitable (but hypothetical) gender performance towards approving spectators, the actor trusts that all those who understand the nature of gender and theatrical performance will applaud the performance and sensibly let her/him go without expecting the offer to be acted out.

209–220 By addressing the audience as if they were 'characters' in a little playlet called 'Epilogue', the actor suggests the parallel with what the spectators have been doing throughout the performance: transforming the stage performers into characters, helped of course by the text and by the actors themselves. This last little demonstration includes creating a 'scene' between this actor and the men and women in the theatre (ll. 209–17), who are given roles and a little scenario to perform in collaboration with her/him.

220 Music to accompany the exit is likely to be used. There may or may not also be a brief encore of the wedding dance (or of a different one as a kind of curtain call), depending on what sort of last theatrical statement is desired.

Juliet Stevenson, who played Rosalind in 1985 (see below, pp. 136–9), spoke of the ending of the performance in this way: 'I don't expect audiences to go skipping out of *As You Like It* humming the tunes, because the play isn't about that' (Rutter, 1988, p. 121). For her, the issues incorporated in the play were paramount and she hoped 'the audience [would] go out of the theatre talking to each other' about the play (ibid., p. 121). However the performance is ended, the actor playing Rosalind has the task of establishing a final relationship with the audience, which includes both playful celebration and thoughtful teasing.

4 Key Productions and Performances

Background

The stage history of *As You Like It* doesn't properly begin until the eighteenth century. Until then, the play seems to have been neglected, or, if there were performances, they remained unrecorded. In 1723, as previously mentioned, a pastiche version of the play, called *Love in a Forest*, was staged at the Drury Lane theatre. This kept the main plot of the play, but dropped Touchstone, Audrey, William, Phebe and Corin altogether. Oliver and Orlando argued using the words of Bolingbroke and Mowbray from *Richard II*, while the mechanicals from *A Midsummer Night's Dream* appeared in the Forest of Arden to perform Pyramus and Thisbe for Duke Senior while Rosalind was changing costume for her wedding. Jaques was in love with, and in the end married to, Celia. This 'mingle-mangle' seems to have been created to give the stars of the Drury Lane company – Colley Cibber (Jaques), Barton Booth (Duke Senior) and Mrs Booth (Rosalind) – an opportunity to perform choice roles and moments from the play. The piece ran for only six performances. A more or less complete version of the play was performed in 1740 at the Drury Lane, with Hannah Pritchard as a very popular Rosalind and the much-loved Kitty Clive as Celia. The performance was interspersed with songs and dances and followed by a pantomime, *Robin Goodfellow*. During the 1740s and 1750s, Peg Woffington, who had been applauded in 'breeches parts' for much of her career (see Brissenden, 1993, pp. 54–5, for useful comments on the popularity of these transvestite roles), played Rosalind, making her farewell appearance in the part in 1757. Dorothy Jordan was another very successful Rosalind, appearing in the role many times from 1787 to 1814, and famous for her sprightly and 'hoydenish' performance.

The play continued to be very popular throughout most of the nineteenth century, mainly because of a succession of highly success-ful Rosalinds (though Jaques and Touchstone were also frequent choices by a number of famous actors), but also because it offered an inviting opportunity for the kind of picturesque scenery which more and more dominated the nineteenth-century stage. Lavish forest settings became standard for the play, with a charming, graceful Rosalind (never convincingly male, lest the actress's sexual attrac-tiveness be compromised) adorning the leafy stage and the most famous male actors enjoying the opportunities for foolery and eccentricity offered by Touchstone and Jaques. One of the most famous nineteenth-century Rosalinds was Helen Faucit, who performed the role from 1839 to 1866, rendering the character more romantic and feminine than her renowned and playful predecessor, Dorothy Jordan. Faucit introduced touches like surreptitiously kiss-ing the chain from around her neck before giving it to Orlando (Carlyle, 2000, p. 286), and, at the end of the mock wedding, falling into a state of dreamy abstraction before finally rousing herself with 'a merry laugh' (ibid., p. 290). Other famous nineteenth-century Rosalinds were Mary Anderson (at Stratford in 1885 and in New York in 1888), Ada Rehan (New York 1889 and London 1890) and Lily Langtry (1890).

The play's popularity continued into the new century, with two tendencies becoming apparent. The first was an increasing emphasis on the visual potential of the play. Early in the century, in a continu-ation of the nineteenth-century pictorial approach, more and more realistic detail was used. The charm of the Forest of Arden was often enhanced by the addition of striking rustic touches: one famous example is the use of a real stuffed stag for Act IV, Scene ii, which became an annual fixture – more and more moth-eaten – in Stratford productions between 1879 and 1919. (This scene has proved to be a temptation for many directors: see, for example, Peter Stein's handling of the scene, mentioned below). For a long time, it was virtually obligatory to transform the stage into a convincing forest. In a production at His Majesty's Theatre in 1907, for example, Oscar

Asche filled the stage with 'a collection of moss-grown logs, two thousand pots of fern, large clumps of bamboo, and leaves by the cartload from the previous autumn' (Trewin, 1964, p. 47). Autumn leaves seem to have been a particularly popular means of creating a sylvan environment: Frank Benson, in his Stratford productions between 1910 and 1919, covered the stage ankle-deep in leaves for his actors to wade through noisily (Beauman, 1982, p. 65).

Twentieth-century advances in scenic and especially lighting technology made elaborate representations of Arden's magic even more attractive to directors and designers. It became common to enhance the transformative mood of Arden with variegated 'forest' lighting in the style of Adolpe Appia, as, for example, in a 1936 Prague production using expressionistic projections of leaf patterns, or in the use of dappled sunlight through the leaves of a giant oak in Michael Elliott's 1961 production. A common approach involved turning the stage into a place only symbolically forest-like, a neutral but evocative space where 'magical' things could happen. Designers sometimes moved beyond any specific attempt to represent the mood or milieu of a forest into more formalist approaches. In 1936, for example, Esmé Church used settings in the style of Watteau, while Clifford Williams's all-male production in 1967 had a a setting by Ralph Koltai 'which transformed Arden into . . . a dream-space of modern art . . . in the form of hanging Plexiglass tubes and abstract sheets cut out of a metal screen' (Kennedy, *Looking at Shakespeare*, 1993, p. 258). In 1977, Trevor Nunn produced a version which rendered the play as a baroque 'opera'. Duke Frederick's court consisted of monochrome flats and the Forest was full of paper snowflakes, until spring came in the form of paper flower petals.

The second tendency in twentieth-century productions of the play – particularly in the decades following the Second World War – was for a directorial 'concept' to dominate the staging. While *As You Like It* continued to present opportunities for outstanding performances by actors (still mainly in the Rosalind role), in an age when reverence was no longer the usual attitude towards Shakespeare, the text was more and more frequently cut and/or rearranged to match a particular approach and to exploit the technical capabilities of the modern theatre. The result was that the physicalities of the staging sometimes rivalled or even conflicted with the mimetic experience of the text. An extreme but interesting example was a production by the Romanian director Petrica Ionescu, in Bochum, Germany, in 1976. Using an all-male cast, the play was performed in a set suggesting, in the words of one critic, 'a vandalized slaughterhouse or a war-damaged factory, with burst pipes, torn-off tiles, and heaps of rubble' (Kennedy, *Foreign Shakespeare*, 1993, p. 235). Rosalind and Celia and most of the other characters were played by muscular male actors behaving like tough infantrymen, the production's underlying concept being that 'a group of hard-boiled soldiers, survivors of an atomic war, [were] killing time by performing a comedy they could not understand any more, since women and love had been dead for a long time' (ibid., p. 237). As with many 'concept'-dominated productions, a deliberate, supposedly dialectical conflict was created between the text and the staging.

It is interesting that directorial concepts have often focused on the setting, the idea being that the particular scenic approach would provide not only an appropriate environment for the characters, but even a kind of visual expression of the 'meaning' of the play. This tendency was perhaps a consequence, at least in part, of the enduring influence of the expressionistic theatre of the early twentieth century, in which scenery and lighting were often designed as almost abstract expressions of the characters' inner feelings, notably the subconscious fears and desires found in dreams. The love story and supposed magicality of the setting have invited subjective interpretations of *As You Like It*. The main plot of the play has often been seen as essentially a traditional 'fairy tale' (for example, by Terry Hands in his 1980 production: see *Players of Shakespeare 1*, p. 67), and the very fluidity of the Forest of Arden as locale has served to justify some kind of expressionistic indeterminacy.

One interesting index to the variety of approaches to staging the play in recent decades is provided by the different treatments of the Hymen figure, an element which particularly invites interpretative and stylistic freeplay. Whereas in Elizabethan times Hymen would almost certainly have been a formally costumed figure in a metatheatrical masque, many modern directors have sought to find a way of making him a mysterious, magically significant figure. In John

Caird's 1989 production, for example, he was 'a strong man in a green costume with an angel perched on his back, leading two children by the hand' (*Players of Shakespeare 3*, p. 84). Peter Stein in 1977 had emphasized the deliberate artificiality of the play's ending by bringing on a gilded Hymen in an ornate tunic and shirt, drawn on a 'wedding wagon' (Patterson, 1981, p. 147). In the same year, Trevor Nunn (in a way reverting to a stylized Renaissance approach) had an elaborately gowned Hymen mounted on a two-dimensional cloud. Perhaps the most purely expressionistic Hymen was that created by Adrian Noble for his 1985 production: he was presented, first, as 'a flickering silhouette on a lighted screen' (*Players of Shakespeare 2*, p. 70), and later, in London, as 'a mere beam of light whose source was *behind* the audience' (ibid., p. 70).

Perhaps the most notable tendency of recent productions has been to look for every possible opportunity to theatricalize the play, that is, to find the most conspicuously theatrical staging for a scene, a character, or even a moment. The wrestling scene, an obvious opportunity for such treatment, has sometimes been expanded into a virtual show in itself. In John Caird's 1989 production, for example, Duke Frederick entered like a mafia *capo* and, when the bout began, some of the actors joined the audience in the stalls, encouraging them to join in shouts and boos. At the end of the match, Orlando signed autographs, posed for photographs and received a huge trophy; then, when he spoke his father's name, Frederick's thuggish bodyguards suddenly appeared, putting on sunglasses and drawing their pistols (see Holland, 1997, pp. 56–7).

All in all, the imaginative freedom of the play's action in its later Arden scenes has proved an incentive for directors and designers to engage in comparable freedom in the staging. Just as the Forest was seen to provide an escape from the reality of everyday life, the play itself was taken as an opportunity to escape traditional stage realism – quite apart from the fact that the text was not written for realistic staging in the first place. More and more, as directorial 'concepts' dominated productions, the play was seen as having some definable 'meaning'. In this curious way, a theme – or at least a director's idea of the play – became the main determinant of a production's approach. The effect upon actors' work was often to encourage more 'unified' and subjective interpretations of character and action (see, for example, the comments of Juliet Stevenson and Fiona Shaw in *Players of Shakespeare* 2, p. 55ff). Another consequence of the emphasis on 'concept' has been a tendency to focus on the visual aspects of the staging, sometimes to the detriment of other elements. Juliet Stevenson herself (who played Rosalind in Adrian Noble's 1985 production) speaks of the danger in giving too much attention to visual and physical staging:

> If you make a decision to impose a stage image on Shakespeare's language – there is a trend towards a dependence on the visual image at the expense of the verbal imagery created by the language – or if production choices set a different rhythm to the one the language is setting, you may be creating trouble for yourselves.   (Rutter, 1988, p. 100)

As always, the problem facing directors, designers and actors has been to find the right balance for their time and place between the text and the physical presence of a theatrical performance. Some of the ways recent productions have tried to do this are discussed below.

Key recent productions

Over the last five decades, productions of *As You Like It* (as with other Shakespearean plays) have on the whole ceased to be reverential 'realizations' of the Bard's immortal words and become collaborations, with the play's text and the directors' and actors' contributions regarded as more or less equal in importance. Five productions suggest some of the more striking theatrical approaches to the play: Michael Elliott's 1961 production with Vanessa Redgrave; Peter Stein's 1977 production at the Schaubühne am Halleschen Ufer in West Berlin; Adrian Noble's Stratford production in 1985; Cheek by Jowl's 1991 all-male performance directed by Declan Donnellan; and Lucy Bailey's staging of the play at the Globe Theatre in 1998. Each of these focused on some particular aspect of the play's performance potentiality, while at the same time giving comparatively free rein to the creative responses of director, designer and actors.

The scenery for Michael Elliott's production for the National Shakespeare Company was a modernist–symbolist version of the romantic forest which had dominated nineteenth- and early twentieth-century performances. It consisted of 'a swelling green knoll above which grew the stylised tree that was Arden' (Trewin, 1964, p. 247): that is, a giant oak through whose leafy (or bare) branches clear or speckled light (depending on the season) fell upon the actors beneath. The setting was strongly lyrical while suggesting to one reviewer 'an outsize production of *Waiting for Godot*' (*Sunday Times*, 9 July 1961; quoted by Brown, 1979, p. 238). The rest of the production seems also to have been in the romantic tradition, making the play 'a Brothers Grimm type of fairy tale' for one critic, while for another it created 'the sadness implicit in a tale of precarious happiness snatched from misfortune' (quoted by Latham, 1975, p. xc). Accordingly, the production became a vehicle for the charismatic actress in the Rosalind role, Vanessa Redgrave. She 'was no carefree, confident Rosalind, stage-managing affairs in the forest, but a waif who unsealed springs of pathos in the part, her gaiety and courage the more admirable because a little tremulous' (Latham, 1975, p. xc). Her performance provoked ecstatic responses from (largely male) critics. According to one, she 'created the spring as she moved' (Trewin, 1964, p. 247), while another wrote, 'Miss Redgrave . . . smiles away all problems, striking a silver note unheard on our stage for years: a note which sings of radiance without effort' (*Sunday Times*, 9 July 1961; quoted by Brown, 1979, p. 239). The ultimate praise came from *The Times*'s Bernard Levin, who wrote – without apparent embarrassment – that she was 'a creature of fire and light, her voice a golden gate on lapis lazuli hinges, her body a slender reed rippling in the breeze of her love. This is not acting at all,' he adds, 'but living, being loved' (quoted by Cook, 1980, p. 19). Aside from such pure adulation, what is striking about some critical responses to this production was their tendency to equate this particular aspect of the main role with the 'true' Shakespearean intention: the *Birmingham Mail*'s critic, for example, wrote that *As You Like It* 'has had to wait until the 1960s for someone to appreciate that this is what Rosalind is' (quoted by Owens and Goodman, 1996, p. 234).

Peter Stein's production in West Berlin's Schaubühne am

Halleschen Ufer was the culmination of a long period of research and experimentation. Stein and his colleagues had for several years been engaged in a project exploring Elizabethan life and thought, along with the work of Shakespeare. This was brought to fruition in the presentation of a kind of 'living museum' at the CCC film studios in Spandau in December 1976. Given an English title, 'Shakespeare's Memory', it presented two evenings consisting of a great variety of exhibitions and performances, including morris dancing, fencing, musical performances and folk theatre (a mummer's play and *The Second Shepherd's Pageant*), as well as brief performances of set pieces from Shakespeare's plays, including *The Winter's Tale, Macbeth* and *A Midsummer Night's Dream*. These were acted in a variety of styles, no attempt being made to give a full performance, since the company preferred to wait for their forthcoming production of *As You Like It* to present their fully worked out style of performance.

'Shakespeare's Memory' had the advantage of giving Stein's company experience in performing in the promenade style, to which they were entirely unaccustomed, which forced them to play close to and even in direct confrontation with spectators. Their research into the Elizabethan period also helped them in approaching the performance of Shakespeare in general, though they did not explore many aspects of Elizabethan staging which might have seemed more immediately relevant to this play, such as clowning and the boy players.

After much discussion, Stein and his company decided on *As You Like It* as the play they would produce. Stein had reservations about the play, however, which he admitted was 'totally foreign' to him, 'so full of ideas, so complex and so lacking in consistency that he for one found it hard to come to terms with' (Patterson, 1981, p. 133). After a difficult rehearsal period, the production, again staged in the CCC film studios rather than the company's usual theatre, opened on 20 September 1977. The first part of the play was performed in a long hall with platforms on three sides. On these, as the audience entered and remained standing, the actors sat immobile (except for a silently weeping Rosalind), dressed in rich Elizabethan costumes. The first section (including I.i, I.ii, I.iii, II.ii, II.iii and III.i) was presented cinematically, with cross-cut segments, between which actors stood frozen while another segment was performed. Instead of the play's fairly formal verbal exposition, the audience were given a passage of filmic montage, with the effect, as one reviewer put it, of 'interweaving the various plots and character fates so that their dilemmas are witnessed in immediate confrontation rather than in reflection' (quoted in Patterson, 1981, pp. 134–5). The expositional material spoken in the original text by Charles and Oliver was given to two lords, who walked among the spectators conversing as if on a crowded London street. Charles was played by a powerful heavyweight professional wrestler (his lines spoken by Le Beau in the third person) and the bout with Orlando (in a loincloth) was the highpoint of the first part of the performance. The movement was so polished and practised that it seemed almost like the staged wrestling matches now seen on television, but Stein seems to have intended the artificiality as appropriate to the rigid formality of Frederick's court. The same quality was displayed in the acting of the first part: Oliver was a melodramatic villain, Adam an almost parodic stereotype of an old man. Touchstone became a pathetic, pudgy, infantile clown, sulkily sucking his thumb. Only Rosalind broke through this studied formality, performing with a lively variety of feelings. The stilted playing seems to have been a conscious directorial choice, intended to make the court so uncomfortable and oppressive for the audience that the only sufficient response was to seek escape, as Rosalind, Celia and Orlando finally do. The first part of the performance ended with Duke Frederick's order for Oliver to find Orlando, at which the amplified barking of hunting dogs reverberated through the hall and Oliver and his servants went out through a door in one of the walls.

The audience were invited to follow, and filed out of the hall into a dim labyrinth, the walls dripping with water, artificial creepers hanging from above. This winding passageway contained various collages on the walls, and other curious displays from the 'Shakespeare's Memory' exhibition of some months before. As the sound of hounds gradually decreased, it was replaced by hunting horns from Arden. The passage from one setting to another was intended to be, for the spectators, a move from the brutal formality of the court to a kind of re-birth in the spatial freedom and innocence of the forest.

The forest setting, designed by Karl-Ernst Herrmann, was a complete woodland environment created in the huge film sound stage. The main acting area was open, surrounded and backed by an elaborate forest setting: the sound of birdsong and music, golden light from above, some falling through the leaves of an enormous beech tree (transplanted from a forest on the outskirts of Berlin), a shallow pool of water, on one side of which was a field of corn. The forest environment was further enhanced by suspending tree trunks around the studio and filling empty spaces with foliage, artificial grass and various rural objects, such as a loom, a butter churn and a rowing boat. An electric organ was mounted against a pillar to one side and provided occasional background music.

The audience were seated in a horseshoe-shaped ring around a large central playing space of about 40 by 100 feet, with additional acting areas on raised catwalks on the walls of the studio, in the aisles between the seats and on several raised platforms, later to serve as Audrey's home, the farm cottage Rosalind and Celia purchase, and Duke Senior's courtly 'campsite'. As the various scenes of the play were played in these areas, other persons and activities continued throughout the performance: for example, lords arranging their flower or butterfly collections, Audrey churning butter, a hunter firing a live round from his rifle (causing leaves to flutter down). There was so much activity that it was impossible to see everything in a single performance: a witch-like figure kept appearing at odd moments, a hair-covered hermit occasionally rushed along a catwalk muttering to himself, a straw man came and went. Robin Hood also made an appearance, as did Robinson Crusoe shouting for his Man Friday. The setting provided an entire performance of its own, a rendition in stage terms of forest life in all its strangeness and innocence, though the interspersed appearances of odd figures were timed so as not to distract from the important dramatic scenes.

The physicality of the setting was underlined in the handling of such scenes as the short scene (IV.ii) in which the Lords celebrate the killing of a deer. In Stein's production, they carried in a slain deer and proceeded actually to skin it and drape the hide over one of the Lords, after which they performed a primitive hunting dance. As the lights dimmed, Rosalind and Celia fell asleep in each other's arms and

Orlando was seen painting his face like a woman. He was confronted by the figure covered with the deerskin and they engaged in a violent struggle (prefiguring Orlando's reported fight with the lion), while Rosalind and Celia, still locked in each other's arms, rolled across the stage. (Stein made no attempt to explain this sequence, calling it 'a dreamlike mime sequence' with no 'narrow interpretable significance' (Patterson, 1981, p. 145), but others have remarked on its erotic symbolism, seemingly derived in part from Jan Kott's famous essay 'Bitter Arcadia' (see pp. 157–8, below), which was reprinted in the Schaubühne programme.) Equally violent was the crashing entrance at the end of the play by a dozen armoured knights representing Duke Frederick's invasion of Arden. As they hacked their way through the forest, they were overpowered by some magical force, finally throwing off their armour and collapsing on the ground or into the pool.

The acting in general was simple and relaxed, but with no attempt at psychological realism. Two years earlier, Stein had already expressed his view of how the play should be acted: 'It is impossible to approach these events in a psychological manner, because they cannot be played that way.' He wanted, as Brecht had suggested many years earlier, for his actors to find 'something more theatrical, treat it like some kind of sport (for example, a boxing match)' (ibid., 1981, p. 142). Accordingly, his actors performed playfully and irreverently, emphasizing situation rather than individual psychological motivations. The relationship between Orlando and the teasing Ganymede, including the mock wedding, were played like children's games, only childishly flirtatious. Equally contemptuous of realistic psychology, Stein had his Celia and Oliver falling into each other's arms over the swooning Rosalind. 'How do you know how quickly Oliver and Celia fall in love or what Shakespeare intended?' Stein asked. 'His play is full of even more incredible incidents' (ibid., 1981, p. 146).

At the end of the play, it was Jaques – who had throughout the action wandered about as a disinterested observer in the background – who remained in Arden, the only character not caught up in the illusion of the forest and therefore the only one who did not have to leave. After the arrival of the gilded Hymen in his wagon, the other characters (excepting Jaques) changed back into the court dress of the opening act. As they engaged in a final formal dance, they approached the far end of the forest area, finally to be hurled off into the cold world of the court once more. Meanwhile, Corin began to clear up the debris left in the forest by civilization: the abandoned weapons, clothing, armour; and the audience saw Duke Frederick, having discarded his armour, lying at the foot of the great beech tree, proclaiming 'The Cycle of the Seasons', a prose poem by the French writer Francis Ponge in which the inevitability of seasonal rotations is summarized, expressing Stein's own view that the freedom of nature is an illusion.

A criticism sometimes levelled at the performance was that Stein's vision was unclear and incompletely formulated. Certainly the production had such complexity and richness – even confusion – as to represent an imaginative experience of the almost limitless suggestions of the play, rather than a coherent directorial 'concept'. We must assume that it was just this lack of logical clarity that Stein wished to convey. After all, he had earlier admitted that he and his company 'approached Shakespeare as we would a great continent, and perhaps our navigational means were not adequate; maybe the boats were too small and the sails too big' (ibid., 1981, p. 132).

The Adrian Noble production, with scenery and costumes by Bob Crowley, opened at the Stratford Shakespeare Theatre on 11 April 1985, moving to London in the autumn, with some changes. The cast included Juliet Stevenson as Rosalind, with Fiona Shaw as Celia and Alan Rickman as Jaques. The opening scene was played in front of a grey curtain, which, as the scene ended, was gusted away, revealing what one actor called 'a memory place', a large room suggesting an attic or storage space, filled with furniture and other large objects covered with dust sheets. This space served for the rest of the play, being a place which evoked a sense of personal memory and imagination and lent itself to transformation. At first, the space had been conceived as a place of escape for Rosalind and Celia, a kind of attic or nursery where they could 'find refuge and thereby create . . . an imaginative world of their own' (*Players of Shakespeare* 2, p. 58). It is this decision which started the use of the stage as representing a subjective, expressionist place. 'We decided as a company,' Juliet

Stevenson says, 'to explore the possibility that Arden could be created in such an attic, with dust sheets twisted into trunks of trees and spreading like canopies of leaf, chests becoming tree stumps, and so on' (ibid., p. 58). The convention of having actors change the setting themselves by handling stage props and scenic pieces was used – here begun when Rosalind tugged at a dust sheet and revealed a mirror underneath, in which, wrapping herself in the sheet, she contemplated herself. At the end of Rosalind and Celia's first scene, the 'attic' was abruptly filled with men limbering up for the wrestling matches. Subsequently, Duke Frederick entered in military evening dress, carrying a brandy snifter, and the 'attic' became a gentlemen's club, a potentially dangerous setting for the young women. With the end of the Duke Frederick scenes, the change to the Forest of Arden was accomplished by Duke Senior (played by the same actor as his brother) entering through the same mirror-frame, with the same courtiers now deployed as his brother's attendants, dust covers now pulled over their shoulders against the cold of the wintry forest ('the icy fang / And churlish chiding of the winter's wind' (II.i.6–7)). Rosalind, Celia and Touchstone entered Arden pulling long coils of white parachute silk, which spread out to cover the stage as they trudged about before collapsing in exhaustion.

After the interval, Arden became green. The clock and mirror were still on stage, now cased in green, and a stream – a natural mirror – now crossed the stage, with the parachute silk hung above the stage like a symbolic copse. The performance ended with a dance, at the end of which – the other performers still on the stage – Rosalind delivered the Epilogue. When the production was moved to London, it was decided that this was too confusing for the audience, and the other actors left the stage through a moon-like opening at the back and Rosalind – now alone on the stage – addressed the spectators.

The production was partly based on several ideas of Karl Jung (some of whose writing was reprinted in the programme), notably those of the psyche consisting of male and female (*animus* and *anima*), and of dreams being structured like plays, with shifting, fluid places and identities. Noble's directorial concept amounted to 'a kind of staged unconscious, where role-reversal was the norm' (Holmes,

2004, p. 149) and where 'court and country, sinner and saint, cynic and convertite and, above all, man and woman were implied to be merely opposite sides of the same coin' (Shrimpton, *Shakespeare Survey*, 39, 1986, p. 200). In its development of feeling states, the production created not so much a dramatic as a psychological landscape. Stevenson and Shaw describe the forest as 'both an image from our nightmares and a place of infinite potential. Above all, we felt, it is a metaphor' (*Players of Shakespeare* 2, 1988, p. 63). In performance, however, they found so abstract an interpretation too problematic, and often fell back on playing the text as it expressed the impulses of the moment.

These two actors' approach to their roles, however, remained in many ways psychological and ideological, based on their own friendship and on an incisive and thoughtful feminism. Stevenson saw Rosalind as experiencing a kind of voyage of discovery. 'I don't think she knows any of what she discovers in herself *before* she finds it in Arden. But I think she has the most profound yearning' (Rutter, 1988, p. 98). She also saw her character as complemented by Celia. 'Rosalind draws strongly on Celia's presence; to show off, outrage, seek refuge in, and silently confer with – as it is often possible to be braver with your best friend at hand, and as the presence of an observer frequently does afford greater freedom, rather than less' (*Players of Shakespeare* 2, 1988, p. 67). The Rosalind–Celia relationship, like that between the two actors, was close and intense, but not without conflict. The difficulties of the Celia role were considerable: the end of Act I, scene ii, for example, when Celia says to Rosalind, 'I'll go along with thee' is 'the end of Celia's play', says Shaw (Rutter, 1988, p. 103). The growing separation between the two characters – from the point when Rosalind first falls in love with Orlando – became an important element in the development of the action. When, at the end of Act IV, scene i, Celia berates Rosalind for 'misusing our sex' and Rosalind for the first time addresses her as 'Aliena' (IV.i. 205), it seems to 'set the seal on their divide', Shaw remarks. 'Rosalind has now abandoned all sensibility in relation to her cousin, and Celia is alone.' After this, Celia is ready for a love of her own: she is 'now available, and readiness is all' (*Players of Shakespeare* 2, 1988, p. 69). The emotional grounding for Celia's and Oliver's precipitous falling in love in the swooning scene (IV.iii) is well laid out by this interpretation.

Jaques too was carefully conceived by Alan Rickman, who saw him as 'more than a famous speech on legs' (ibid., 1988, p. 75). To Rickman, Jaques was 'the entertainer, the radical, someone to wind up. Good value' (ibid., p. 76). He noted too that it was Jaques who initiated the conversations with Touchstone, Orlando and Rosalind and he was the one who 'when disarmed, runs away. Therein lie both his vulnerability and his arrogance' (ibid., p. 78). Yet Rickman's playing of the scene when the armed Orlando bursts in on the forest dinner, declaring that 'he dies who touches any of this fruit, / Till I and my affairs are answered' (II.vii.99–100), created a memorable moment. 'And you will not be answered with reason, I must die' (II.vii.101), Jaques replied, walking silently to the table, picking up an apple and biting into it.

The production created numerous other highly theatrical moments. The wrestling match became a veritable circus and the final wedding scene ended in a glorious dance by the entire company, at the end of which the actors in 'a moment of still suspension . . . took in the *consequences* of the return to the ordered world . . . then exited, through a moon-shaped hole in the backdrop' (ibid., 1988, p. 71).

Stevenson expressed the whole approach of this production when she spoke of how she and the others wanted the play to end for spectators:

> I don't expect audiences to go skipping out of *As You Like It* humming the tunes, because the play isn't about that. It isn't about confirming cosy opinions or settled stereotypes. It isn't about a woman in search of romantic love. The search is for knowledge and faith, and in that search Rosalind is clamorous – as clamorous as "a parrot against the rain"!' (Rutter, 1988, p. 121)

Declan Donnellan's Cheek by Jowl production, after opening in 1991, proved so popular that it was re-opened in 1994 and taken on a world tour through the following year, offering (according to Mel Gussow in the *New York Times*) 'an answer to sceptics who still believe the old canard that the English are stuffy about their Shakespeare'

(*New York Times*, 26 July 1991, C18). The play was performed with an all-male cast, though in a very different style from that used in Clifford Williams's 1967 all-male production, which had, according to a programme note, tried to create 'an atmosphere of spiritual purity which transcends sensuality in the search for poetic sexuality' (cited by Latham, 1975, p. xci). Donnellan's production made no attempt to transcend the physical, but celebrated it, creating what one critic called an 'unabashed celebration of gay desire ... and homosocial bonding' (Bate and Jackson, 1996, p. 6). It was by no means, however, merely a display of camp homosexuality. Indeed, as John Peter pointed out, 'Declan Donnellan's production reveals that *As You Like It* is not about sexuality (hetero-, homo-, bi- or trans-) but about love, which transcends sexuality and includes it' (quoted by Holland, 1997, p. 92). While some saw the all-male casting as yet another example of masculine colonialism, in its elimination of women from theatrical representation, for others 'gender became a construct of performance' and 'performing gender became a game (as when Orlando playfully punched Ganymede's arm and Rosalind awkwardly returned the male gesture, though the actor could easily have punched him back)' (ibid., p. 91). The gender of a character was thus sometimes linked to the gender of the actor and sometimes not.

The production was frankly theatrical throughout. Donnellan began the performance with his entire cast on stage, all in black trousers, white shirts and black braces. Jaques started his 'All the world's a stage / All the men and women merely players', using the last words to divide the actors into male and female characters. The whole company remained on stage during the first sequence, watching each others' performances. The stage itself was a simple wooden box, adorned with green pennants hanging from the flies to designate Arden. Individual character costumes were created by token items added to the basic black and white. Adam wore a bowler hat and Rosalind a white headband, while Audrey wore a mini-skirt and a long yellow wig (and yodelled for her goats). Corin had a strong Northern accent, smoked a pipe and spoke Every. Word. Very. Carefully. From time to time the actors played jazz. In Act V, scene iii, Touchstone, Audrey and the two (adult) pages snuggled beneath a blanket, Touchstone trying to keep Audrey from the pages' grasp as they all sang 'It was a lover and his lass', eight bare feet waggling in rhythm to the tune.

Despite the jocularity of much of the stage business, Donnellan was trying to suggest something violent beneath the surface of the play. There was a considerable element of despair in Jaques, presented as a sterotypical 'camp' gay man, perpetually trying to seduce young men while constantly voicing his bleak pessimism about humankind and the emptiness of human life. At the end, he is ironically paired off with Hymen. The Celia–Rosalind relationship was full of tension. In the first scene, they were presented as lovers and Celia was embittered by Rosalind's sudden love for Orlando. When they reached the forest, she hoped for reconciliation, but was further angered by Orlando's reappearance. She spent much of the time thereafter wandering about in disconsolate jealousy, waiting for her own Mr Right, who finally appeared in the person of Oliver. The playing between Orlando and Ganymede was erotically charged without becoming explicit or camp. Sharply disappointed that he did not recognize her when they first met in the forest, Rosalind made the intensity of her feeling fully clear in the following scenes: it was love rather than mere sexuality, however. One of the production's most telling moments came at the end when Rosalind lifted her bridal veil and offered herself to Orlando. Shocked at having been deceived, he turned on his heel and stalked off to the back of the stage. It was only after several moments, filled with other stage action, that he finally returned, in control again, accepting her and more in love than ever, and Rosalind drew him into a passionate embrace.

The production's high theatricality culminated in a joyous and bizarre carnival-like ending, some of the actors playing jazz as everyone danced. In some performances, the house lights were brought up before the Epilogue. The audience's enthusiastic applause was interrupted by Adrian Lester as Rosalind, who gestured to the spectators to stop clapping and then spoke the Epilogue with ingratiating charm, giving some a clearly homoerotic charge with his offer, 'If I were a woman' (*laughter*) . . . 'I would kiss as many of you' (lines 214–15). As the performance ended, the consensus seems to have been, as one critic remarked, that 'the play's joyousness [was] fully accepted and expressed by the company' (Holland, 1997, p. 94).

Lucy Bailey's production opened at London's Globe Theatre in 1998. Though an outstanding production for a variety of reasons, it was of particular interest because it was played in a replica of the theatre in which the play was first staged in 1600. The theatre was adapted in some details for a modern production, but tried to use the space in essentially the same way as the original performances might have done, though making sometimes over-conscientious efforts to include the whole theatre and the audience. The stage floor was covered with sheepskins. A half curtain was hung between the pillars of the stage, which were draped with the skeletons of saplings; ladders were placed against the upper stage, steps led down from the front of the forestage to the yard (through which many entrances and exits were made) and musicians (providing not only music but bird-song) were scattered about the stage and auditorium galleries.

The performance began in front of the half curtain with a dumb show, accompanied by the singing of a ballad in the yard, of the story of old Sir Rowland de Boys, who took leave of his three sons before slumping dead in his chair. The theatre yard was used for the violent wrestling scene, as well as for the later mime of the killing of a deer. Conscious of the vast space of the Globe that had to be filled, the actors gave physically vigorous performances. Phebe, a husky country lass with more of Touchstone's 'Jane Smile' (II.iv.43–53) about her than of delicate pastoral maiden, pursued Ganymede up a ladder and almost off the edge of the stage, while Rosalind's desperate effort to get rid of her 'doublet and hose' (III.ii.215–16) gave spectators a flash of bare buttocks. Touchstone and Audrey engaged in a broadly farcical strip tease during 'A lover and his lass' (V.iii), while at the end of the mock wedding, Rosalind gave Orlando a prolonged kiss which left him gasping – though none the wiser about her identity. Similarly, Celia seized and kissed Oliver over the body of the swooned Rosalind (IV.iii).

The resolution of the plot was handled with deliberate emphasis on the cocky arbitrariness of Rosalind's management of people and events, which was performed playfully to the audience for what it was: a convenient way of wrapping up the play. The final ceremony, conducted by Hymen – a thin, elderly man in little more than a loin-cloth – was given an air of serious solemnity, however, emphasized by the ringing of the bell in the canopy above the stage. As intended, the performance had the air of a carnival noisily celebrated in a very public theatre, perhaps the most appropriate way to play *As You Like It*.

It is interesting that the basic architectural shape of the Elizabethan public theatre has been increasing in popularity in recent theatre-building. More and more acting companies have found the freedom and direct audience contact encouraged by this arrangement of stage and audience spaces liberating for their work – by no means only the plays of Shakespeare. Some years ago, the small Swan Theatre was added to the large barn-like Memorial Theatre at Stratford-on-Avon and more recently Peter Hall was the moving force behind the opening of the Rose of Kingston, modelled on the original Rose Theatre which lasted from 1592 to 1603. The new theatre, in which 1000 spectators can be seated in comfortable proximity to the acting area, was appropriately opened in December 2004 with a production of *As You Like It*.

5 The Play on Screen

Film

The stage popularity of *As You Like It* and the opportunity it provided
for pastoral picturesqueness led to several silent film versions in the
early twentieth century, though the idea of making films of
Shakespearean plays did not readily occur at first. In New York, in the
early years of the twentieth century, 'nickelodeons' became enormously popular places to watch early 'movies'. These shabby little
places showing five-cent films of a generally sensational nature (for
example, the drugging of the famous Evelyn Nesbitt in *The Great Thaw
Trial*) were virtually mobbed by eager viewers, and (like the early
Elizabethan theatre companies) aroused much anger among the
city's moralists. On Christmas Eve 1908, in response to their protests,
the Mayor of New York shut down 500 nickelodeons, officially on
the grounds that they were firetraps.

Fortuitously, it was in the same year that the first film version of
As You Like It had appeared. An open-air version made by the Kalem
Company, it was a very truncated affair showing only a few famous
scenes. More elaborate versions were to follow. At about the same
time, the film-making Vitagraph Company decided to produce a
series of more 'elitist' one-reel films, hoping such fare might compete
with the nickelodeons. Vitagraph's adventurous entrepreneur, J.
Stuart Blackton, proceeded to turn out a number of 'quality' motion
pictures designed to attract a 'classier' audience. These included films
about George Washington (including the famous crossing of the
Delaware River with his bedraggled troops in the Revolutionary
War), Dante's Francesca da Rimini, and stories from the Bible. The
most highbrow of Vitagraph's offerings was a series of films of

Shakespearean plays, most of which highlighted already famous scenes like the assassination of Julius Caesar or the balcony scene from *Romeo and Juliet.*

In 1912, Vitagraph produced a 30-minute version of *As You Like It.* The role of Rosalind was played by Rose Coghlan, who had first performed the part with modest success on stage in 1880, but who was now 61. Her husband, Charles Coghlan, had played Hamlet in New York and had had some success in London, but her own career was declining, which may have motivated her to make one last attempt at immortality on film. Sadly, like so many silent film performances in those early days, hers is a grainy parody of bad stage acting, and even the background greenery looks drab in black and white. This is the last of the silent films of the play, with the single exception of a modern-dress version made in 1916 by the London Film Company, of which prints are unfortunately virtually inaccessible.

The story of sound film versions of *As You Like It* is also distressingly short. The first was a major film enterprise, costing the then enormous sum of $1,000,000, made for 20th-century Fox in 1935 by the well-known Hungarian-born director Paul Czinner. The star was Czinner's wife, Elisabeth Bergner, Polish-born and with a brilliant film and stage career in Austria and Germany behind her. Her Orlando was Laurence Olivier, at the time a rising young ingenu of the London stage. Bergner and Olivier were both criticized for their acting, though (even with her Continental accent) her Peter Pan style of playing the role received more positive response than his rather glum performance. (Fifty years later, he complained that the sheep 'ran away with the film' – Olivier, 1986, p. 177.)

Czinner's version took full advantage of the medium's resources, however, to give the story some visual liveliness. The leading actors are viewed from every possible angle – two-shot, over-the-shoulder, close-up and many other camera set-ups. Bergner executes countless lively bits of business to enhance the film: whirls, turns, giggles, even the occasional somersault. The wrestling scene includes a blow-by-blow account by Touchstone as he mimes and reacts to the wrestlers' groans and grunts, assisted by the London Philharmonic's playing of William Walton's energetic score. The film ran only 97 minutes and therefore cut a number of scenes, including the Sir Oliver Martext marriage preparation and Touchstone's seven-lies set-piece in the final scene. As it ends, the film removes any of the play's darker subtext by cutting Jaques's final speech, and Bergner's delivery of the Epilogue steals the show, as she teasingly brandishes her favourite switch at the audience, before magically dissolving into a vision in a white, virginal gown as she flatters the men in the audience.

The only other full-length film version of the play was in a very different style. It appeared in 1992 and was directed by Christine Edzard, who had done an award-winning *Little Dorrit* four years before and had worked with Franco Zefferelli. Aside from the technical limitations imposed by a low budget and the difficulties in understanding the actors' idiosyncratic speech, the film's main difficulty for viewers has arisen from the choice to set the action in a derelict, rubbish-strewn vacant lot on the East London waterfront. Duke Frederick's court is an adaptation of an abandoned bank lobby, while his brother Duke and his Lords huddle outdoors around an oil drum brazier. Jaques' Seven Ages of Man speech is used to start the film, though the speaking of James Fox, dressed in a shabby black hat and overcoat, brings little life to the famous set-piece. Other well-known actors have similar difficulties. Griff Rhys Jones as Touchstone adopts a virtually impenetrable regional accent, while the usually excellent Cyril Cusack gives Adam inappropriate theatricality. The greatest success in the film is enjoyed by the young actors playing the lovers. Emma Croft brings great energy and bounce to Rosalind, as she leaps and cavorts around the vacant lot which stands in for the Forest of Arden. Andrew Tiernan (doubling as Oliver) plays Orlando with verve, chalking up his love poems on derelict wooden fences. Unfortunately, the low budget seems to have been the cause of great difficulties with the sound: being under the Heathrow flight path combined with a background urban rumble enhances neither intelligibility nor romantic atmosphere. But the ending is surprisingly effective: a mist rolling in from the river just as the nuptials are to begin underlines the director's aim of contrasting the easy dreams of romance with the harsh realities of life. Though rough, the film gave a surprising breath of life to a play too often prettified on both stage and screen.

Television

There have been several televised versions of the play. An 11-minute excerpt, broadcast by the BBC on 5 February 1937, was the first ever televised Shakespeare. Based on Act III, scene ii of the play, it featured Margretta Scott and Ion Swinley. The first full television production of the play, aired on 14 July 1946, was directed by Ian Atkins, with Vivienne Bennett as Rosalind, John Byron as Orlando and David Read as Jaques. A more elaborate attempt, broadcast on 13 March 1953, was a television adaptation of Glen Byam Shaw's Stratford production of the previous year. The cast of this version consisted of established stage and film stars of the day: Margaret Leighton, Laurence Harvey and Michael Hordern. On 22 March 1963, a television adaptation of Michael Elliott's highly praised Stratford production of 1961 (see above, p. 131) was shown. The cast included Vanessa Redgrave, Patrick Allen and Max Adrian and was directed by Ronald Eyre.

The most serious attempt at putting the play on television was a part of the BBC series which set out to televise all of Shakespeare's plays. Directed by Basil Coleman, this version of *As You Like It* was broadcast on 17 December 1978. Helen Mirren played a rather serious, quizzical Rosalind, with Richard Pasco as a sour, alcoholic Jaques. In both cases, the actors' performances may have been affected by the swarms of midges that attacked the cast as they valiantly struggled to play comedy in the long grass of the park of Glamis Castle in Scotland. The location was chosen by the series producer, Cedric Messina, apparently with the idea that a picturesque natural location would best suit the play's supposedly idyllic setting. Even if there had been no midges, however, the use of a single location fixes the action and the characters in a single real-life place, with none of the flexibility of the stage and possessing too strong a presence of its own to allow the free play of such a variety of characters as are found in *As You Like It*.

It is striking, especially in view of the great popularity of *As You Like It* in the theatre, that there have been so few screen versions of the play. Perhaps its very theatricality has defeated attempts to film or televise it. Both these media may be too realistic for the imaginative flexibility of *As You Like It*, nor do they – despite the claims of some film theorists – allow enough of the right kind of intimacy with the characters, for the intimacy of the actor on stage is a very different thing from that of a screen close-up. The characters of *As You Like It* seem to require a different kind of emotional distance from what is possible on the screen. Their flexible and subjective reality, as the BBC television version made clear, is of a very different kind from the camera-never-lies 'truth' of film and television. Another reason why the play seems to resist screen treatment may be the nature of its supposedly 'definitive' locale. As has already been suggested, the Forest of Arden does not lend itself to realistic presentation. It remains an essentially subjective element, an almost neutral arena for the characters' actions and a reflection of their attitudes. Even more: for much of the play, once the atmosphere of Arden has been established, the physical setting simply does not play a very important role. Yet in the screen media – aside from close-ups, which hardly seem appropriate to the ironic, theatrical distance of *As You Like It* – the background usually has a very strong presence as part of the film medium's fundamental attempt to persuade viewers that they are watching reality. Recalling Olivier's remark about the sheep that 'ran away with the film', we remind ourselves that the 'reality' of *As You Like It* is the theatre.

For this reason, video versions of theatrical productions, whose purpose is to record the reality of a stage performance, rather than fictional 'life', may be the best way to view the play on screen. Fortunately, there are videotapes of recent productions available through the Royal Shakespeare Company. In addition, there is a BBC/Open University video (1995), titled *As You Like It*, produced and directed by Amanda Willett. This includes student workshops, interviews with actors and directors, extracts from the Cheek by Jowl production and an extract from the banishment scene (I.iii) played by student actors and directed by Fiona Shaw.

6 Critical Assessments

Early criticism

Given the fact that, after its initial Elizabethan performances, *As You Like It* was not staged again until 1740, it is not surprising that no criticism of the play appears earlier. (In fact, there is little Shakespearean criticism even of a general kind until well into the eighteenth century.) Among the earliest critical remarks on the play are those in David Erskine Baker's *The Companion to the Playhouse*, published in 1764, only twenty-four years after the first performance since the time of Shakespeare. In that interval, the play quickly gained popularity, apparently because of its escapist charm for both spectator and reader, as Baker's comments suggest:

> It is, perhaps, the truest pastoral drama that ever was written; nor is it ever seen without pleasure to all present. In the closet it gives equal delight, from the beauty and simplicity of the poetry.　(quoted in Brown, 1979, p. 25)

Another critic of the time, the eminent Samuel Johnson, suggests a further reason for the play's popularity: the basic preference of his age for comedy over tragedy. In the preface to his edition of the works, Johnson comments that Shakespeare's tragedy has the 'great appearance of toil and study', whereas his comedy is natural and unforced. 'His disposition . . . led him to comedy. . . . In comedy he seems to repose, or to luxuriate, as in a mode of thinking congenial to his nature. In his tragic scenes there is always something wanting, but his comedy often surpasses expectation or desire' (ibid., p. 27). Johnson's approval of Shakespeare's comedies, including *As You Like It*, is based on his view that his characters 'act upon principles arising

from genuine passion . . . their pleasures and vexations are commu-
nicable to all times and to all places; they are natural and therefore
durable' (ibid., p. 27). Specifically of *As You Like It*, Johnson had this to
say:

> Of this play the fable is wild and pleasing. I know not how the ladies will
> approve the facility with which both Rosalind and Celia give away their
> hearts. To Celia much may be forgiven for the heroism of her friendship.
> The character of Jaques is natural and well preserved. The comic dialogue
> is very sprightly, with less mixture of low buffoonery than in some other
> plays; and the graver part is elegant and harmonious. By hastening to the
> end of his work, Shakespeare suppressed the dialogue between the
> usurper and the hermit and lost the opportunity of exhibiting a moral
> lesson in which he might have found matter worthy of his highest
> powers.   (ibid., p. 28)

Typically for an age when the rational was celebrated even above the
natural, Johnson cannot refrain from commenting on Shakespeare's
failure to seize an opportunity for moralizing, regardless of literary
or theatrical criteria.

The tendency of the dramatic criticism of the early nineteenth
century was more towards the idealistic–literary than the theatrical.
Even a sophisticated critic like Hazlitt wrote less of Shakespeare's
dramatic constructions as such (much less as performances), than of
the ideal creations to be found in them. Thus in *Characters of
Shakspeare's Plays* (1817; 3rd edition 1838), *As You Like It* is described as

> the most ideal of any of this author's plays. It is a pastoral drama, in which
> the interest arises more out of the sentiments and characters than out of
> the action or situations.   (quoted in Brown, 1979, p. 33)

Of the Forest of Arden Hazlitt says, 'The very air of the place seems to
breathe a spirit of philosophical poetry' (ibid., p. 33). He is equally
romantic in his approach to the characters, who, 'within the
sequestered and romantic glades of the forest of Arden . . . find
leisure to be good and wise, or to play the fool and fall in love' (ibid.,
p. 34). Jaques is 'the only purely contemplative character in
Shakspeare . . . the prince of philosophical idlers' (ibid., p. 33).

'Rosalind's character is made up of sportive gaiety and natural tenderness', to which 'the silent and retired character of Celia is a necessary relief' (ibid., p. 34). While he was at times a perceptive and sensitive theatrical critic, Hazlitt none the less wrote of the play as essentially a literary fiction, representing a higher reality than stage performance could ever fully realize. This approach to Shakespeare as a dramatic poet rather than a crafter of plays persisted in criticism throughout the nineteenth and well into the twentieth century, having its effect not only upon readers but upon stage productions as well, which tended to focus on pictorial idealism and a beautiful, lovable Rosalind.

Modern criticism

The nineteenth-century fascination with Shakespeare's characters continued in the criticism of the twentieth century. As the century turned, many critics, encouraged by a reaction against Naturalism, came to mistrust plot as a merely mechanical manipulation of events. Character criticism continued to figure large in commentaries on Shakespeare's individual plays, including *As You Like It*, as it has virtually to the present day. Important books on the subject contained useful insights into the play, for example John Palmer's *The Comic Characters of Shakespeare* (1946), but, despite their other concerns, many critics continued to engage in extended interpretations of the fictional characters of the plays, virtually as if they were characters in novels. Even in reviews of stage productions, the focus on character remained a dominant strain. The power of the actors' presence in the theatre makes this understandable, perhaps, but the result was that theatrical criticism often failed to view the performed play as a total theatrical structure. In the case of *As You Like It*, this has contributed to a persistent tendency to view the play as little more than a gallery of charming, lovable characters.

In the second half of the century, however, most serious academic criticism of *As You Like It* went further, becoming engaged with such matters as genre and the play's dramatic structure, as well as the ideas embodied in it. A number of critics have explored Shakespeare's

themes in the play. One influential example is Jay L. Halio's essay,
' "No Clock in the Forest": Time in *As You Like It*'. 'In *As You Like It*,' says
Halio, 'Shakespeare exploits timelessness as a convention of the
pastoral ideal. . . . Although neither will quite do, timelessness in
Arden (on the whole) contrasts favorably to the time-consciousness
of court and city life. . . . In addition, timelessness links life in Arden
with the ideal of an older, more gracious way of life that helps regen-
erate a corrupt present' (Halio, 1968, p. 388). In Arden, the young
gentlemen around Duke Senior 'fleet their time carelessly as they did
in the golden world' as Charles remarks (I.i.101). Touchstone
expresses the opposing attitude, brought from the court, and his
view is 'shared by the malcontent Jaques, his fellow satirist, and in
some respects by Rosalind. Touchstone is, in fact, the play's time-
keeper, as Harold Jenkins has called him, and his most extended
disquisition on time is fittingly recounted by Jaques (II.vii.20–8)'
(ibid., pp. 93–4). Throughout the play, argues Halio, Shakespeare
contrasts the timelessness of the forest world with the time-ridden
preoccupations of court and city life. Rosalind's sense of time is very
different from Touchstone's obsession with 'riping and rotting'
(II.vii.26–7) and from the view laid out in Jaques's Seven Ages speech.
His famous monologue, describing a man in his time playing many
parts, is a 'series of vignettes illustrating the movement of a person *in*
time. Rosalind not only adds appreciably to Jaques's gallery, but
showing profounder insight, she shifts the emphasis from the movement *of a person*, to the movement *of time*' (ibid., p. 95). Her version
accounts more thoroughly for *duration*, or the perception of time.
Rosalind's time consciousness, in general, says Halio, goes beyond
the mere moment: 'She knows the history of love – witness her
speech on Troilus and Leander (IV.i.94–108) – and she predicts its
future, as she warns Orlando of love's seasons after marriage
(IV.i.143–9)' (ibid., pp. 95–6). Her ardent love, he continues, is in
comic juxtaposition with her realistic insight, just as Orlando's self-
conscious dress and unawareness of punctuality contrast comically
with his poetic protestations of love. 'Were it not for Rosalind, he
might, like Silvius, linger through an eternity of unconsummated
loving' (ibid., p. 96). Finally, argues Halio, Rosalind 'remains a
primary agent for the synthesis of values that underlies regeneration

in Shakespeare's comedy. . . . With regard to time she moves with Orlando to a proper balance of unharried awareness. For all of these functions – as for others – the timeless world of the forest, with its complement of aliens, serves as a haven; but more importantly, it serves as a school' (ibid., p. 96).

The theme of order was another subject of Shakespearean criticism, most often discussed in relation to the tragedies and history plays. Its importance in comedy, and in *As You Like It* in particular, was the primary subject of John Russell Brown's *Shakespeare and His Comedies* (1957). In Brown's view, the ending of *As You Like It* represents 'the fullest celebration of the ideal of love's order. As "still music" sounds, Hymen is drawn mysteriously to this place and time, and links earthly and heavenly harmony' (Brown, 1957, p. 141). Then, 'when wonder has become more familiar, when the eight lovers have taken hands, and when news has come of the tyrant duke's abdication', there is music and they dance. 'The exceptional celebration of this conclusion – its formal groupings, music, song, dancing, and attendant god – suggests that *As You Like It* is informed to an exceptional degree by Shakespeare's ideal of love's order' (Brown, 1957, pp. 141–2).

Comparative studies of dramatic types have also contributed importantly to our understanding of the play by clarifying the differences between comedy and the other major genres of drama. The groundwork for this approach was laid by Northrop Frye in *A Natural Perspective* (1965). Frye's study made use of the traditions of dramatic type deriving from Greek drama (including Aristophanic comedy) and stressed the functional nature of character. In addition to the better known classical types of the *eiron* (ironist), *alazon* (boastful pretender) and *bomolochos* (buffoon or clown), Frye noted the presence of another comic type, represented in *As You Like It* by Jaques. This type is linked with the clown and 'personifies a withdrawal from the comic society. [This character] is usually isolated from the action by being the focus of the anticomic mood . . . [or may be] simply opposed by temperament to festivity, like Jaques' (Frye, 1965, p. 93). Importantly, adds Frye, this figure is not a character type, like the clown – though there can be resemblances – 'but a structural device that may use a variety of characters' (Frye, 1965, p. 93).

While stressing the function of comedy to achieve reconciliation between conflicting forces, Frye also pointed out a counter tendency involving a contrast between the individualizing movement of comedy and the impulse towards incorporating social identity into that of the group. This contrast, he points out, corresponds to a split in the mind of the spectator. As the comedy formulates the creation of a new society, the audience are invited to participate in this society and in the festive mood it generates. Characters who obstruct or oppose the new society are usually ridiculed. While the majority of the characters advance, in the final scene, towards the new society and join it, there is also 'in any well-constructed comedy . . . a character or two who remain isolated from the action, spectators of it, and identifiable with the spectator aspect of ourselves' (ibid., p. 92): in *As You Like It*, this is Jaques. The effect, Frye argues, is that 'part of us . . . if we like the comedy, feels involved with the new society and impelled to participate in it; but part of us will always remain spectator, on the outside looking in' (ibid., pp. 91–2). The comic dramatist has to be alert to this ambivalence in his audience.

A particularly influential example of the generic approach to Shakespearean comedy – and particularly *As You Like It* – was C. L. Barber's book *Shakespeare's Festive Comedies* (1963), which, as its subtitle indicated, was 'A Study of Dramatic Form and Its Relation to Social Custom'. Shakespeare's comedy, Barber asserts, is 'saturnalian', because it participates in native celebratory traditions of popular theatre and popular holidays. His interest is in how the social form of Elizabethan holidays contributed to the dramatic form of festive comedy. One important source was the theatrical institution of clowning. The clown figure, like his ancestor the Vice, was 'a recognized anarchist who made aberration obvious by carrying release to absurd extremes' (Barber, 1963, p. 5). It is significant, for Barber, that Shakespeare's first truly masterful comic scenes were written for the clowns. But, he adds, the festival occasion provides the fundamental form.

The release provided by what Barber calls the 'idyllic comedies', such as *As You Like It*, is accomplished by making the whole experience of the play like that of a revel. This is achieved by directly staging pastimes, dances, songs, masques, plays extempore, and so on.

But the fundamental method, says Barber, is to shape a loose narrative so that events put its characters in the position of festive celebrants. Rosalind's 'mock wooing with Orlando amounts to a disguising, with carnival freedom from the decorum of her identity and her sex' (ibid., p. 6). To translate festive experience into drama involved exploring the sort of awareness traditionally associated with holiday, and also becoming conscious of holiday itself in a new way. 'The plays present a mockery of what is unnatural which gives scope and point to the sort of scoffs and jests shouted by dancers in the churchyard or in "the quaint mazes in the wanton green" ' (ibid., p. 8). This is not satire of the usual kind. Satirical comedy, Barber makes clear, portrays the relations between social classes and aberrations in movements between them. Saturnalian comedy is only incidentally satirical, however, its primary target being 'perverse hostility to pleasure'. 'Highflown idealism is mocked too, by a benevolent ridicule which sees it as a not unnatural attempt to be more than natural' (ibid., p. 9).

Barber regards it as unfortunate that a play like *As You Like It* has come to be known as a 'romantic comedy', since what the play actually does is to establish a humorous perspective towards the fanciful hyperbole of Renaissance romances, whose 'wishful absolutes about love's finality . . . are made fun of by suggesting that love is not a matter of life and death, but of springtime, the only pretty ring time' (ibid., p. 9). Rosalind's realism about love, Barber adds, is 'a recognition of the seasons, of nature's part in man, [though this] need not qualify the intensity of feeling in the festive comedies' (ibid., p. 9). While the conventional romances of the time attempted to create intensity by elaborate hyperbole based on 'a pretty, pseudo-theological system', a comedy like *As You Like It* expresses the power of love as 'a compelling rhythm in man and nature' (ibid., p. 9).

Another kind of criticism which has addressed itself particularly to *As You Like It* has been source study, which is concerned mainly with examining Shakespearean plays in terms of how they made use of their sources. An important value of this kind of study is its provision of information about contemporary material Shakespeare may have known about or made use of. Such examinations can reveal much about the date and historical context of a play (including the ways in which it differs from other work of the time). Even more important, however, is what it indicates about the dramatist's way of working, revealed in the choices and changes he made in the materials he used. The most influential figure in Shakespearean source study has been Geoffrey Bullough, whose *Narrative and Dramatic Sources of Shakespeare* (1957–75), in eight volumes, collects and examines all the known and likely sources of Shakespeare's plays. Bullough's examination of Shakespeare's use of Lodge's *Rosalynde* suggests some important points about how the play was constructed (see above, pp. 122–4). Shakespeare approached his sources in two ways, says Bullough. First, he used them as repositories of incidents, '*lazzi*', plots and personages. At the same time, they were the sources of 'themes', by which Bullough means general motifs he could manipulate in the process of re-creation. 'In *Rosalynde*', says Bullough, 'he seems to have discovered a theme which may be broadly described as the opposition between Fortune and the Good Life, between Nature and Artifice, between the manners of the Court and those of the Country' (Bullough, 1963, vol. 2, pp. 150–1). In his use of the pastoral, Shakespeare, not liking the artificial when it takes itself seriously, lifts Coridon (in Lodge, the old wise shepherd of Virgil and Spenser) out of the group of pastoral lovers and creates round him a new set of characters, Audrey, William, Sir Oliver Martext. These new characters, when combined with Touchstone and his wooing of Audrey, reveal what country life, country people and country love are like at their most 'natural'. Bullough believed that in doing so Shakespeare took hints (and Corin's name) from an old play which may also have been in his mind when he was writing *Twelfth Night* and maybe even *Hamlet*. This was *Sir Clyomon and Clamydes*, written 1570–90 and printed in 1599, in which the princess Neronis, escaping in man's dress into the forest from the King of Norway, meets Corin, a shepherd, and takes service with him (ibid., p. 155). Bullough also speculates that Shakespeare may have got his title from Lodge's address 'to the Gentlemen Readers' – 'if you like it, so' (ibid., p. 160). 'Maybe,' says Bullough,

> for they liked that sort of thing well, as Shakespeare had already proved, and he liked it himself. It is incredible that *As You Like It* would have been

the play it is if he had been contemptuous of his material and his audience. Maybe he thought a title relatively unimportant, and he knew that
the public would find an elusive, impertinent one attractive.   (ibid.,
p. 157)

A distinctive contribution to twentieth-century Shakespeare criticism was the Polish critic Jan Kott's *Shakespeare Our Contemporary*
(1965), which had a considerable influence on both critics and theatre
practitioners in the 1960s and thereafter. Kott's criticism is a stimulating blend of imaginative scholarship and theatrical knowledge-
ability. In his chapter on *As You Like It* and *Twelfth Night*, entitled
'Shakespeare's Bitter Arcadia', Kott writes about the interplay
between Orlando and Rosalind as Ganymede: 'The disguise is a
masquerade. A masquerade, too, has its eroticism and its meta-
physics' (Kott, 1965, p. 213). He mentions Aretino's *Dialogues of
Courtesans*, in which the teachers advised their adepts to disguise
themselves and pretend to be boys, the most effective means to rouse
passion. Kott is particularly perceptive when he writes of the
Ganymede–Orlando love game, reminding us that we can understand certain things about these scenes better if we remember the
aesthetics of Genet (especially perhaps in a play like *The Blacks*). To
Genet, theatre is the image of human relationships not because it
more or less successfully represents them, but because 'it is based on
falseness; original falseness, rather like original sin. The actor plays a
character he is not. . . . To be oneself means only to play one's own
reflection in the eyes of strangers' (ibid., p. 218). In the forest love
scenes, adds Kott, 'the "real" girl is the disguised boy' (ibid., p. 218).
Reminding us that Rosalind was played by a boy actor playing a girl
playing a boy playing a 'girl', Kott describes the situation as being 'real
and unreal, false and genuine at the same time. And we cannot tell on
which side of the looking glass we have found ourselves' (ibid.,
p. 219). He goes on to assert that the love scenes have the logic of
dreams: 'Plans, persons, tenses – past, present, future – are intermingled; so is parody with poetry' (ibid., p. 219). This kind of dream, says
Kott, is 'a dream of erotic experience in which one is one's own partner, in which one sees and experiences sensual pleasure, as it were,
from the other side. One is oneself and at the same time someone

else, someone like oneself and yet different' (ibid., p. 220). But, importantly, he adds, such disguise arouses 'a dream of love free from the
limitations of sex; of love pervading the bodies of boys and girls, men
and women, in the way light penetrates through glass' (ibid., p. 221).

Kott's recurring motif is the coexistence and confrontation of
opposites, which he sees as stemming from Renaissance thought and
the realities of Renaissance staging. Works like *As You Like It* and
Twelfth Night are conceived in the spirit of Ariosto, with a combination of pathos and irony, mockery and lyricism. This mixture Kott
regards as very modern. Also modern, even closer to our own time,
is 'the ambiguous attitude to madness; or rather, to the escape into
madness, into mythology and into disguise' (ibid., p. 226).
Shakespeare has no illusions, Kott asserts, not even the illusion that
we can live without illusions. 'He takes us into the Forest of Arden in
order to show that one must try to escape, although there is no
escape; that the Forest of Arden does not exist, but those who do not
run away will be murdered' (ibid., p. 227). (Interestingly, Kott suggests
that at the end of the play Jaques stays in Arden because he is the only
one who can live without illusions: 'he is the only one who has no
reason to leave the forest because he has never believed in it, has
never entered Arcadia' – ibid., p. 231.) In his emphasis on the ironic
doubleness of Shakespeare's vision in the play, Kott also wants to
undermine the traditional simplistic view of romantic comedy. 'Of
all the "contemporary reactions" to Shakespeare,' he says, 'from
Elizabethan times to ours, the romantic was the most false and the
one that left behind it the most fatal theatrical tradition' (ibid., p. 229).

A particularly active area in Shakespearean criticism has been that
which focuses on the political implications of the plays and derives
interpretations from a study of their contemporary political context,
as well as their place in present-day culture. The single most important single figure in the genesis of political criticism (or 'materialist'
criticism, as it is now sometimes called) was of course Karl Marx,
though nowadays few critics regard themselves as merely Marxists.
The emergence in the 1980s of New Historicism marked a significant
step in the evolution of materialist criticism, reflecting the influence
of the French Marxist Michel Foucault, who shifted from Marx's
focus on the economic to a concern with the functioning of power in

cultural practice. In 1980, Stephen Greenblatt made a crucial contribution in his *Renaissance Self-Fashioning: From More to Shakespeare*, in which he explored the almost theatrical creation of a 'public personality' as an instrument of political power (Elizabeth I being a prime example), including the 'scripting', 'rehearsal' and 'performance' of appropriate activities by this persona in the course of exercising that power. At about the same time, the Marxist critic Raymond Williams exerted considerable influence on Shakespearean criticism with his interpretations of culture – significantly including drama – as a site of social struggle, in such books as *Problems in Materialism and Culture* (1980). With regard to specific plays, Williams's heirs have concentrated much of their attention on how the socio-political structures of Elizabethan society are expressed in dramatic characters and action. Respecting *As You Like It*, much interest has been shown in the functioning of rank and class in the play. When characters of the aristocratic class come to the Forest of Arden, for example, they continue to exercise their 'natural' superiority over the 'natives', their social inferiors. Thus Rosalind and Celia condescend to Corin, Silvius and Phebe, while Touchstone, a would-be courtier, lords it over Corin, Audrey and William. Duke Senior establishes a facsimile-court, founded on aristocratic assumptions of a 'natural order', where he and his lords dress up as 'foresters' and 'outlaws' while maintaining all the attitudes and behaviours of their class. Central to the materialist interpretation is an awareness of the profoundly hierarchical socio-political structure of Elizabethan–Jacobean England, which underlies the worlds of *As You Like It* and, though disrupted by Oliver and Duke Frederick, is restored at the end by a series of convenient 'magical' transformations. The formal ceremonies and dances with which the play concludes, they argue, are therefore to be seen as celebrations of the restoration of the 'natural' or God-given power structure of society.

The heirs of Raymond Williams among present-day critics, the 'cultural materialists', also devote their attention to how Shakespeare and Shakespearean drama function today as parts of a national cultural establishment centred around 'The Bard of Avon', expressed in such prestigious institutions as the Royal Shakespeare Theatre and Stratford-on-Avon as a virtual theme park with its swans, theatres and tea-rooms. The enduring popularity of *As You Like It* arouses suspicion in such critics, justified by productions which present the play as a celebration of all that is 'pretty' and 'charming' in the sacrosanct Shakespeare 'canon'. The play's continued popular success, according to Mary Hamer, has been due largely to 'the idealization of the feminine and the seduction of the audience' (Hamer, 1986, p. 117) through sentimental portrayals of Rosalind.

The utilization of Rosalind as a supposed icon of 'femininity' is a subject of particular concern to another important school of Shakespearean study, feminist criticism. A comparative newcomer in Shakespearean studies, feminist criticism has now been a significant voice for several decades. Its concern is not merely with the representation of female characters in the plays, but with the deeper and more complex subject of gender relations and behaviour, in both historical and dramatic/theatrical contexts. The feminist approach takes on added interest in the context of Elizabethan theatrical performance, because of the presence of boy players in female roles, which complicates the representation and thus the interpretation of gender behaviour. This element, together with the dynamic and volatile changes occurring in the relations between men and women as the sixteenth century was coming to an end, has made the comedies involving gender disguise, such as *The Two Gentlemen of Verona*, *Twelfth Night* and *As You Like It*, particularly interesting subjects for feminist critics. In these plays, which are focused in the traditional comic way on getting their female characters to the altar, gender issues of crucial importance are raised, including not only marriage, but also inheritance, property ownership, language and social relations. The treatment of these matters is rendered even more interesting by the equivocal gender identity of the masquerading heroine. This ambiguity gives rise to many opportunities for gender-related issues to be tied in with questions of identity and of the nature and function of theatrical performance. The matter of language, too, as both a sign and a determinant of gender, also comes into play, as, for example, in the question of the relative 'femininity' and 'masculinity' of the language employed by Rosalind and Orlando. Studies have revealed that in much of the play 'her' language employs more 'masculine' idioms and structures than 'his': 'What traditionally is made to characterize feminine discourse is irrationality, chaos and fragmentation, but Rosalind's text is characteristically male' (Reynolds, 1988, p. 85). Another consideration brought into play by feminist criticism is the question of stage identity, particularly complex in plays written for boy actors in female roles. As Catherine Belsey points out, *As You Like It* 'can be read as posing at certain critical moments the simple, but in comedy unexpected, question, "Who is speaking?" ' Particularly in the Epilogue, this is a question that 'elicits no single or simple answer' (Belsey, 1985, pp. 180–1). The final scene of the play arouses other, even broader questions, combining feminist with socio-political concerns. It resembles *The Taming of the Shrew* and *A Midsummer Night's Dream* in how it obliterates the possible female disruption of the gender status quo by means of a resolution that 'magically reconciles rebellious "feminine" and individualist desire to a rigid social hierarchy of aristocratic and patriarchal privilege' (Kavanagh, 1985, pp. 155–6).

Perhaps the most influential tendency in modern Shakespearean criticism has been what is usually called 'performance criticism', which is based on a reading of the plays as texts for the theatre. The task of performance critics, according to Miriam Gilbert, is to 'look for every clue [to performance] they can find, and intensive scrutiny of the play-text produces multiple performance texts' (Gilbert, 2003, p. 556). Jonathan Holmes and W. B. Worthen both argue that for performance criticism 'to be really productive, it must learn to exist between the two disciplines of textual criticism and theatrical practice' (Holmes, 2004, p. 178).

Performance criticism dates back to early in the twentieth century, most notably in the writing of Harley Granville Barker (*Prefaces to Shakespeare*, 1927–46), based on his extensive work as an actor and director, and Muriel C. Bradbrook, a scholar who approached the plays with a profound knowledge of Elizabethan theatre practice (*Elizabethan Stage Conditions: A Study of their Place in the Interpretation of Shakespeare's Plays*, 1932). The next stage in the development of performance criticism occurred in the 1950s, with the appearance of several important articles. A particularly influential example was Warren D. Smith's 'Stage Business in Shakespeare's Dialogue' (1953), in which he pointed out the many cues found in Shakespearean dialogue which draw the audience's attention to actors' physical actions. In the following decade, a number of influential books of performance criticism appeared, including Bernard Beckerman's *Shakespeare at the Globe (1599–1609)* (1962). Also influential were J. L. Styan's *Elements of Drama* (1960) and *Shakespeare's Stagecraft* (1967), the latter succinctly stating the primary aim of performance criticism: 'The requirement of Shakespearean scholarship, whether the critic's or the actor's, is first to be able to read the texts through the eyes of an Elizabethan actor' (Styan, 1967, p. 229).

Another important contributor to the development of Shakespearean performance criticism was John Russell Brown. In his *Shakespeare's Plays in Performance* (1966), he laid out some of the basic principles of performance criticism and, while he makes little mention of *As You Like It* (which he discusses at length elsewhere, see References), several of his points are particularly relevant to the play. He warns against the seductive power of the play's language, for example: Shakespeare's verbal art 'is, in fact, a trap; it can prevent us from inquiring further' (Brown, 1966, p. 7). He urges reading the Shakespearean text in terms of its performance requirements and possibilities, studying it as actors and directors would do.

This draws him into a consideration of subtext, a matter some have considered irrelevant to acting Shakespeare. But actors have always looked 'under the words', Brown points out, citing Henry Irving's quotation of his famous predecessor, Macready, who claimed that the actor's task was '*to comprehend the thoughts that are hidden under words*, and thus possess oneself of the actual mind of the individual man' (ibid., p. 53). As Brown remarks, the relevance of this kind of subtext to *As You Like It* is apparent, most obviously in Rosalind, whose underlying feelings are perpetually masked and played out in the indirect mode through an adopted disguise. Her swoon in Act IV, scene iii, and her pretence that it was 'counterfeit', also involve a consideration of subtext. 'In this instance,' adds Brown, 'her inward feelings lag behind the bravery of her verbal performance so that she, in effect, denies her words even as she speaks them' (ibid., p. 59). In practice, Brown points out, textual and performance analysis must go hand in hand: 'We should, as it were, keep the plays in constant rehearsal in the theatre of our mind' (ibid., p. 70).

Since the ground-breaking work of Beckerman, Styan and Brown, performance criticism has continued to grow in importance and frequency, incorporating many different angles of approach, from studies of performance history to studies of the interpretation and analysis involved in producing the plays, as in John Barton's *Playing Shakespeare* (1984), for example. An over-riding purpose of performance criticism has been 'to reclaim the Shakespearean text for performance' (Holmes, 2004, p. 142), and it is therefore appropriate that an important contribution has come from actors themselves, partly in the form of discussions of their work in rehearsing and performing a particular character. This kind of criticism has been comprehensively examined and discussed by Jonathan Holmes in *Merely Players? Actors' Accounts of Performing Shakespeare* (2004). A similar subject is discussed by W. B. Worthen in his *Shakespeare and the Authority of Performance* (1997), in which he suggests that the value of actors' discussions as criticism may be limited if we succumb to 'the enervating polarization of "text against performance" ' (Worthen, 1997, p. 190).

In practice, however, many of the actors writing about their work suggest how often in rehearsal they have been persuaded or even forced to fall back upon the authority of the text as a necessary antidote or at least a complement to their own instinctive performative interpretations. For many Shakespearean actors, 'trust the text' becomes almost a mantra. An example is seen in David Tennant's essay on Touchstone (in *Players of Shakespeare 4*). Baffled by the complexity and inconsistencies in the role, he first tries the traditional psychological approach, in which he takes Touchstone's freewheeling ideas, energy and constant loquacity as 'traits of manic episodes in a bi-polar mental illness. It is perhaps a sort of actor's affectation to think of Shakespearean characterisation in this way, but it helped me to make sense of some of Touchstone's less easily motivated moments' (*Players of Shakespeare 4*, 1998, p. 35). In rehearsal, however, Tennant soon found that such a 'textbook' approach was not productive, so he began for a time to try a purely performative attack, making desperate attempts to find ways of being funny: 'I started trying to throw everything at it. Touchstone became a spinning top chucking off silly voices, silly walks, even acrobatics to try and inject some life' (ibid., p. 39). In the end, however, when this didn't work, he had to 'trust Shakespeare', as other actors have frequently spoken of doing. As a result, he gained what he felt was a clearer perception of how Touchstone (and other characters) might have been created by Shakespeare and could be re-created on the stage: by a process of what could be called a sort of performative *bricolage*. 'I found the only way to deal with Touchstone's apparent contradictions', Tennant concludes, 'was to stop striving for a logical through-line and to play each moment as it arrives. After all, the evolution of any human relationship is far from linear' (ibid., p. 40). The same fundamental point is described more fully by another actor, Harriet Walter: 'You play each scene or each beat, however contradictory, or however incompatible it seems with what has gone before or comes after. You play the moment for its integrity, for what it is' (Rutter, 1988, p. 76). Having done this, the actor – and presumably the audience – have learned that, 'by the end of the play, the character is an accumulation of these separate moments' (ibid., p. 76). What has been trusted in this case is not so much the 'truth' of the Shakespearean text as the appropriateness of the improvisatory method to the construction of comic character and the fundamentally ephemeral nature of theatrical performance and response.

Comments like those of Walter suggest how a subjective, performative approach allows character creation to take place in performance. What she describes is a recognition of the fact that the ultimate understanding of character, whether in rehearsal or during performance, does not occur only in the actor. While Jonathan Holmes is critical of actors' analyses, arguing that 'the introspective manner in which many actors construct character is more often than not fundamentally at odds with how that character is constructed in the script and subsequently reconstructed by the spectator' (Holmes, 2004, p. 17), we must none the less acknowledge that actors' criticism has often helped us to recognize that a play in performance is a phenomenon whose full meaning resides neither in the text, nor in the performer, nor indeed in the spectator, but rather in their dialogic interplay. Juliet Stevenson and Fiona Shaw display at least a partial awareness of this when they discuss how to deal with the wooing scenes in *As You Like It*, in which Rosalind and

Orlando do all the talking while Celia remains a silent spectator. 'In the end,' they write, 'the problem is partly resolved by the fourth player – the audience – whose response to the scene and its glorious revelations inevitably serves to punctuate and shape it' (*Players of Shakespeare* 2, 1988, p. 67). Perhaps ironically, it is the very subjectivity of their experience of performance – a subjectivity parallel to those of the dramatic character and the theatrical spectator – that reminds us that the play in performance as a whole is made up of the interactions of subjectivities, creating a composite dialogic meaning, no single element of which can by itself define the whole. It is this complex of theatrical meaning that performance criticism at its best has helped us to understand.

Perhaps the ultimate form of performance criticism is performance itself. Certainly this was the view of John Barton, who, while he came from an academic background, none the less remarked, 'I never wanted to write a book about Shakespeare because I could only express my views and feelings in the form of individual productions' (Barton, 1984, p. 181). Written criticism and analysis of the Shakespearean text, essential though it is, is bloodless and incomplete without the interpretations and insights acted out physically on the stage with the collaboration of an audience. In a 1967 production of *As You Like It*, the comedian Roy Kinnear performed the role of Touchstone in the style of a music hall comedian. The *Financial Times*'s critic, B. A. Young, expressed amazement at how funny Touchstone's 'tedious jokes' could be 'when delivered straight across the footlights like a true clown' (*Financial Times*, 16 June 1967). Kinnear's performance was a small but significant contribution to Shakespearean criticism.

References

As You Like It, ed. Agnes Latham (London: Methuen, 1975; reprinted 2002).

Barber, C. L., *Shakespeare's Festive Comedy: A Study of Dramatic Form and its Relation to Social Custom* (New York: Meridian Books, 1963).

Barton, John, *Playing Shakespeare* (London: Methuen, 1984).

Baskervill, Charles Read, Heltzel, Virgil B. and Netheriot, Arthur H. (eds), *Elizabethan and Stuart Plays* (New York: Holt, Reinhart & Winston, 1934).

Bate, Jonathan and Jackson, Russell, *Shakespeare an Illustrated Stage History* (Oxford: Oxford University Press, 1996).

Beauman, Sally, *The Royal Shakespeare Company: A History of Ten Decades* (Oxford: Oxford University Press, 1982).

Belsey, Catherine, 'Disrupting Sexual Difference: Meaning and Gender in the Comedies', in *Alternative Shakespeares*, ed. John Drakakis (London: Methuen, 1985), pp. 166–90.

Bradbrook, M. C., *The Growth and Structure of Elizabethan Comedy* (London: Chatto, 1955).

Brissenden, Alan, 'Introduction', *As You Like It*, ed. Alan Brissenden (Oxford: Clarendon Press, 1993), pp. 1–86.

Brown, John Russell, *Shakespeare and his Comedies* (London: Methuen, 1957).

Brown, John Russell, *Shakespeare's Plays in Performance* (London: Edward Arnold, 1966).

Brown, John Russell (ed.), *Shakespeare: 'Much Ado About Nothing' and 'As You Like It', A Casebook* (Basingstoke: Macmillan Press, 1979).

Bullough, Geoffrey (ed.), *Narrative and Dramatic Sources of Shakespeare*, vol. 2: *The Comedies, 1597–1603* (London: Routledge & Kegan Paul, 1963).

Carlyle, Carol Jones, *Helen Faucit: Fire and Ice on the Victorian Stage* (London: Society for Theatre Research, 2000).

Cook, Judith, *Women in Shakespeare* (London: Harrap, 1980).

Daniel, Carter A. (ed.), *The Plays of John Lyly* (Lewisburg: Bucknell University Press, 1988).

Dekker, Thomas, *The Shoemakers' Holiday*, in *Elizabethan and Stuart Plays*, ed. Charles Read Baskervill, Virgil B. Heltzel and Arthur H. Nethercot (New York: Holt, Reinhart & Winston, 1934), pp. 555–91.

Dusinberre, Juliet, 'Pancakes and a Date for *As You Like It*', *Shakespeare Quarterly*, vol. 54, no. 4 (Winter 2003), pp. 371–405.

Fletcher, John, 'Epistle to *The Faithful Shepherdess* (1608?)', in Fredson Bowers (ed.), *The Dramatic Works in the Beaumont and Fletcher Canon* (Cambridge: Cambridge University Press, 1976), vol. 3, p. 497.

Frye, Northrop, *A Natural Perspective: The Development of Shakespearean Comedy and Romance* (New York and London: Columbia University Press, 1965).

Gilbert, Miriam, 'Performance Criticism', in Wells, Stanley and Orlin, Lena Cowen, *Shakespeare: An Oxford Guide* (New York: Oxford University Press, 2003), pp. 550–9.

Greenblatt, Stephen J., *Renaissance Self-Fashioning: From More to Shakespeare* (Chicago: University of Chicago Press, 1980).

Gurr, Andrew, *Playgoing in Shakespeare's London* (Cambridge: Cambridge University Press, 1987).

Halio, Jay L., ' "No Clock in the Forest": Time in *As You Like It*', in Jay L. Halio (ed.), *Twentieth Century Interpretations of 'As You Like It'* (Englewood Cliffs, NJ: Prentice-Hall, 1968), pp. 88–97.

Hamer, Mary, 'Shakespeare's Rosalind and Her Public Image', *Theatre Research International*, 11 (1986), pp. 105–18.

Hattaway, Michael, 'Introduction', *As You Like It*, ed. Michael Hattaway (Cambridge: Cambridge University Press, 2000), pp. 1–68.

Holland, Peter, *English Shakespeares: Shakespeare on the English Stage in the 1990s* (Cambridge: Cambridge University Press, 1997).

Holmes, Jonathan, *Merely Players? Actors' Accounts of Performing Shakespeare* (London: Routledge, 2004).

Kavanagh, James H., 'Shakespeare in Ideology', *Alternative Shakespeares*, ed. John Drakakis (London: Methuen, 1985), pp. 144–65

Kennedy, Dennis, *Looking at Shakespeare: A Visual History of Twentieth-Century Performance* (Cambridge: Cambridge University Press, 1993).

Kennedy, Dennis (ed.), *Foreign Shakespeare* (Cambridge: Cambridge University Press, 1993).

Kott, Jan, *Shakespeare Our Contemporary*, translated by Boleslaw Taborski, preface by Peter Brook (London: Methuen, 1965).

Latham, Agnes, 'Introduction', *As You Like It*, ed. Agnes Latham (London: Methuen, 1975; reprinted 2002), pp. ix–xci.

Lyly, John, *The Plays of John Lyly*, ed. Carter A. Daniel (Lewisburg: Bucknell University Press, 1988).

Marston, John, *The Works of John Marston*. ed. A. H. Bullen, 3 vols (London: John Nimmo, 1887).

Mucedorus, in *Elizabethan and Stuart Plays*, ed. Charles Read Baskervill, Virgil B. Heltzel and Arthur H. Nethercot (New York: Holt, Reinhart & Winston, 1934), pp. 525–52.

Nashe, Thomas, *Pierce Pennilesse, His Supplication to the Divell*, in *The Works of Thomas Nashe*, ed. Ronald B. McKerrow, 4 vols (London: Bullen, 1904–8), vol. 1, pp. 137–245.

Olivier, Laurence, *On Acting* (New York: Simon & Schuster, 1986).

Owens, W. R. and Goodman, Lizbeth (eds), *Shakespeare, Aphra Behn and the Canon* (London: Routledge in association with the Open University, 1996), ch. 6: 'Reading *As You Like It*', by Kate Clarke, pp. 193–250.

Patterson, Michael, *Peter Stein: Germany's Leading Theatre Director* (Cambridge: Cambridge University Press, 1981).

Players of Shakespeare 1, ed. Philip Brockbank (Cambridge: Cambridge University Press, 1985).

Players of Shakespeare 2, ed. Russell Jackson and Robert Smallwood (Cambridge: Cambridge University Press, 1988).

Players of Shakespeare 3, ed. Russell Jackson and Robert Smallwood (Cambridge: Cambridge University Press, 1993).

Players of Shakespeare, 4, ed. Robert Smallwood (Cambridge: Cambridge University Press, 1998).

Reynolds, Peter, *Shakespeare 'As You Like It': A Dramatic Commentary* (London: Penguin Books, 1988).

Rutter, Carol with Sinead Cusack, Paola Dionisotti, Fiona Shaw, Juliet Stevenson and Harriet Walter, *Clamorous Voices: Shakespeare's Women Today*, ed Faith Evans (London: The Women's Press, 1988).

Shrimpton, Nicholas, 'Shakespeare Performances in London and Stratford-upon-Avon 1984–5', *Shakespeare Survey*, 39 (1986), pp. 199–203.

Soule, Lesley Wade, *Actor as Anti-Character: Dionysus, the Devil and the Boy Rosalind* (Westport, CT and London: Greenwood Press, 2000).

Spenser, Edmund, *The Fairie Queene*, ed. Thomas P. Roche, Jr (Harmondsworth: Penguin, 1978).

Styan, John L., *Shakespeare's Stagecraft* (Cambridge: Cambridge University Press, 1967).

Thomson, Peter, 'Shakespeare Straight and Crooked: a Review of the 1973 Season at Stratford', in *Shakespeare Survey*, 27 (1974), pp. 143–54.

Trewin, J. C., *Shakespeare on the English Stage, 1900–1964: A Survey of Productions* (London: Barrie and Rockliff, 1964).

Wickham, Glynne, Berry, Herbert and Ingram, William (eds), *English Professional Theatre, 1530–1660* (Cambridge: Cambridge University Press, 2000).

Williams, Raymond, *Problems in Materialism and Culture* (London: Verso, 1980).

Wilson, John Dover, *Life in Shakespeare's England: A Book of Elizabethan Prose* (Cambridge: Cambridge University Press, 1926).

Wilson, Richard, ' "Like the Old Robin Hood": *As You Like It* and the Enclosure Riots', *Shakespeare Quarterly*, vol. 43, no. 1 (Spring 1992), pp. 1–19.

Worthen, W. B., *Shakespeare and the Authority of Performance* (Cambridge: Cambridge University Press, 1997).

Further Reading

Brown, John Russell, *Free Shakespeare* (New York: Applause, 1997). A stimulating little book on approaches to staging Shakespeare today, providing both perceptive criticism and practical advice.

Dusinberre, Juliet, 'As *who* liked it?', *Shakespeare Survey*, 46 (1994), pp. 9–22. A brief and stimulating look at the play from a feminist perspective.

Hayles, Nancy K., 'Sexual Disguise in *As You Like It* and *Twelfth Night*', *Shakespeare Survey*, 32 (1979), pp. 63–72. An intelligent examination of how the use of gender disguise in the two plays creates new sets of meanings.

Jamieson, Michael, *Shakespeare: As You Like It*, Studies in English Literature, No. 25 (London: Edward Arnold, 1965). A brief run through the play with many useful comments.

Palmer, D. J., '*As You Like It* and the Idea of Play', *Critical Quarterly*, vol. 13, no. 3 (Autumn 1971), pp. 234–45. A useful enquiry into how deeply various kinds of playing are imbedded in the play.

Smith, Warren D., 'Stage Business in Shakespeare's Dialogue', *Shakespeare Quarterly*, 3 (1953), pp. 311–16. An early, stimulating look at how text and gesture interrelate in Shakespeare.

Styan, John L., *Shakespeare's Stagecraft* (Cambridge: Cambridge University Press, 1967). One of the most stimulating of the seminal works of performance criticism.

Thomson, Peter, *Shakespeare's Theatre*, 2nd edn (London: Routledge, 1992). The best book on the theatres of Eizabethan London.

Wells, Stanley and Orlin, Lena Cowen (eds), *Shakespeare: An Oxford Guide* (New York: Oxford University Press, 2003). A useful compendium of articles on all aspects of Shakespeare.

Wells, Stanley and Stanton, Sarah (eds), *The Cambridge Companion to Shakespeare on Stage* (Cambridge: Cambridge University Press,

2002). A very valuable look at Shakespearean production from a variety of perspectives, including numerous mentions of *As You Like It*.

Wiles, David, *Shakespeare's Clown: Actor and Text in the Elizabethan Playhouse* (Cambridge: Cambridge University Press, 1987). An invaluable work on the nature, sources and practices of Elizabethan clowns.

Index

2ore gar8alilgisiore waiting

Index

175

Smith, Warren D.
  'Stage Business in Shakespeare's
    Dialogue', 161–2
Spenser, Edmund
  The Faerie Queene, 12, 23
  The Shepheard's Calendar, 16, 23
Stein, Peter, vii, 94, 99, 126, 130,
    131–6
Stephens, John
  Essays and Characters, 9
Stevenson, Juliet, 123, 130, 136, 138, 164
structure of *As You Like It*
  dramatic, 39–42
  theatrical, 43–4
Styan, J. L.
  Elements of Drama, 162
  Shakespeare's Stagecraft, 162

Tale of Gamelyn, The, 24
Tarlton, Dick, 14

Tennant, David, 163–4
Theophrastus
  Characters, 8
Touchstone, 2, 3, 5, 13, 36, 39–41, 45,
    50–1, 63–6, 67, 71, 76–9, 83–6,
    99–100, 107–9, 111, 113–14,
    117–18, 133, 140–1, 142, 145–6,
    152, 156, 159, 163–5

Vice, the, 14, 154

Walter, Harriet, 42, 164
William, 14, 15, 36, 106–7, 109, 156
Williams, Clifford, 127
Williams, Raymond
  Problems in Materialism and Culture,
    159
Worthen, W. B., 161
  *Shakespeare and the Authority of
    Performance*, 163